ISBN 0-937533-89-0
Library of Congress Catalogue Card Number 95-90035

Printed in the USA
First printing 1995
Revised Second Printing 1998

For our Planet,
this book is printed
with soybean ink on
acid free paper.

Published by: Wheel of Life
4511 - Del Rio Road Suite #5
Sacramento, CA 95822

HOW TO READ YOUR OWN HOROSCOPE

TABLE OF CONTENTS

INTRODUCTION 1

1 THE BASICS 5

2 PREDICTION 31

3 ADVANCED PREDICTION 63

4 ALL SLOW TRANSITS 85

5 CASE STUDY 113

APPENDICES

Appendix 1 - The Planets 145

Appendix 2 - The Houses 151

Appendix 3 - Terminology 158

Appendix 4 - Study Exercise Answers 163

Appendix 5 - Ephemeris 166

Astrology will never lie nor deceive. It will give you the absolute truth if you choose to look and have the courage to see.

Timothy Curley

INTRODUCTION

Predicting love, marriage, sex and high or low income times accurately within one month is one of the easiest and most straight forward applications of Astrology. Prediction is so simple, it is quite often overlooked by the professional Astrologer.

In light of this, it's ironic that the following are some of the most frequently asked question a professional Astrologer may hear: When will I fall in love? When will I get married? When will I make a lot of money? When will I have a lover? Why am I having challenges in my marriage now? When will they end and what can I do to resolve them? Once these questions are answered with proven accuracy, the uncertainty revolving around them is automatically removed from your life.

By knowing future conditions you become empowered with the ability to make conscious efforts to resolve past issues. Thus, when the prediction begins to manifest in your life, you shift to a much more satisfying level. The entire process instills in you a true sence of self-mastery.

It would make a lot of sense to ask, "Well, how did Astrologers figure this all out?" It's not like someone sat down one afternoon, started guessing and put this all together. It's literally taken thousands of years to compile the knowledge behind Astrology. And the knowledge is continually growing and expanding. The earliest known records of Astrology are from the Babylonians and date back to about 1645-1625 B.C. The records contain information about the Planet Venus.

This book will show you how to predict in a simple step-by-step format. It presents the information in such a way that you can immediately make accurate predictions. Then, if you choose to refine your predictions, more advanced tools are offered.

Using the basic skills you can predict marriage or commitment, high income and love within 30 days over the entire period of your life. Using the more sophisticated skills you will have the ability to see with certainty the overall conditions under which your predictions will come into your life. You can do this for your family, yourself and your friends. It's simple. But keep in mind as you go along what you are doing. That is, most people live in a fog with regard to future events. You are going to be able to predict major life events within 30 days of their occurrence. As you will find out, this power creates a certain amount of responsibility.

In this book, you will go back in time and look at major issues in your life. Then you will compare these to the Astrological events occurring in your Chart. By following this method of study, you will learn the procedure and prove in a profound personal manner the accuracy of Astrological prediction. Once proven by studying the past, it is an easy step to look forward in time and accurately predict your future.

With the basic prediction method in hand, you will be able to predict major life events quite easily. It is the exciting moment when you clearly see your Astrological predictions manifesting that keeps Astrologers both professional and amateur faithful to the science. The emotionally charged moment when you say, "Wow, it works!" is what has attracted and held people to the study of Astrology for thousands and thousands of years.

It works. Without any doubt at all, it works. This book is designed to get you to that threshold as quickly and easily as possible. It is structured to move you past the veil to the heart of Astrology. It may take you a week or as little as a day depending on how familiar you are with the basics and how much time you have to devote for study. Once you have the exhilarating thrill of saying "It works!" you will be there and will begin your study on a new level.

Because this is a highly condensed, begining Astrological book, many questions should come forward as you study. Write each one down keeping in mind that they will all be answered at the proper time.

It works!

Chapter One

THE BASICS

Not too long ago, in order to learn Astrology, the student had to be quite good with math. The process of producing a Chart required a lengthy amount of time and patience. Before you could even begin the simple techniques of prediction, you had to have an in depth understanding of all the calculations necessary.

The math part of Astrology stood for thousands of years as a veil which would only allow the most motivated to pass through and begin the study. Even math itself was once considered a secret science. But, as we enter into the Age of Aquarius, the New Age, computers have removed this barrier. It is no longer necessary for the new student to spend lengthy amounts of time learning and performing complex calculations in order to do simple but profound Astrological predictions. The math is done instantly by computer. The beginning New Age Astrologer can immediately have all the needed information and then proceed to make profound accurate predictions with only a basic understanding of Astrology.

The modern professional Astrologer either has a computer program to produce the needed information or a computer service which provides Astrological Charts for him. Many professionals, if asked to do the calculations themselves, couldn't. They all use computers.

Prediction is fun and simple. Also, it is absolutely dead accurate. After a short period of time you can amaze yourself, family and friends with your new ability. You will be helping them by offering important information about their lives, which they would not otherwise have. Plus, you will be able to know in advance about things in your life that may have kept you awake at night. Let's say for example you have been concerned because your income has been less than what you need or expected. Using Astrology you will know in advance when income will increase. Having that information can help take the worry out of slow times and give you the opportunity to lay additional groundwork thus increasing income even further at the time when it goes up. Also, knowing in advance when things will be slow will encourage you to save during the better financial periods thus making the slow periods a happier, less stressful time in your life. Or perhaps you have been concerned because you have a friend who has been single for too long. They may want a mate but as yet do not have one. Knowing in advance when the opportunity for commitment will come about opens a window of self-analysis. Knowing in advance relieves pressures created by uncertainty and gives them a chance to focus on issues concerning relationships. Thus, when the event (commitment) occurs they will find it more rewarding and satisfying.

You will need only two things for predicting; this book and a Chart for the person(s) for which you are doing the prediction. If you don't already have a source for Natal Charts, just turn to the back of the book. Because it takes a few days to mail them to you, order them now. That way you can spend the time between learning the fundamentals in this chapter. When your Charts arrive, you'll have everything you need to do your first prediction in Chapter Two! I recommend that you study two Charts minimum; yours and someone you know. Also, unless you are on a tight budget, I recommend "The Works" for yourself. This is a custom package created *specifically* for this book. It includes a 25 to 40 page personalized Ephemeris plus your Chart. It lists all the Planetary information needed on *your* Chart from age ten to ten years after the date of order.

This chapter focuses on the basics needed to get you started with prediction. Then, in Chapter Two there are workbook formatted sections helping you to do your first predictions in an organized, straight forward and accurate fashion. By taking a little time every day to study, you should be able to make your first predictions within a week. Once you've worked through the first two chapters you will be able to predict the exact times of commitment, love and high income for anyone throughout their entire life. Then, as you work into the more advanced study you will be able to refine your predictions.

If you haven't studied Astrology before, take your time. It is important that you try to be clear on the general topics while the details need only be reviewed to gain some familiarity. For example: It's important for you to understand Astrological Houses. But, the exact details of all twelve Houses need not be memorized. Or for example, it's important to have a familiarity with all the Astrological symbols. But, memorizing each symbol is not necessary. Later as you start doing your predictions, all the details will easily fall into place because you will be using the various tables that contain them. By that point, you will probably have them memorized without trying.

As you begin your study, keep in mind that the science of Astrology uses only three things: Signs, Houses and Planets. It is the relationship of those three categories that compose the basis of all Astrology, including Predictive Astrology. Recalling this will help you avoid confusing new details with important basics. As you read you might ask yourself how what you are studying defines or relates to one of the three categories: Signs, Houses or Planets.

THE ZODIAC

Astrologers seek to understand man's relationship to celestial bodies from where he stands. Man stands on Earth. Using Earth as the center gives Astrology a Geocentric perspective (Geo from Greek meaning "the Earth").

From our Geocentric perspective we can look out into space and find twelve star constellations. They are Aries, Taurus, Gemini, Cancer, Leo, Virgo, Libra, Scorpio, Sagittarius, Capricorn, Aquarius and Pisces. As you know these are the Signs of the Zodiac. When Astrology had its beginning thousands of years ago, it was noted that some of the star constellations appeared in the heavens at specific locations as seasons began. It was from this observation and association that the Zodiac Signs received their names. However, over time due to natural changes in the Earth's axial rotations, these famous star constellations no longer appear in the same position in the sky during seasonal changes. But, the Zodiac names and Zodiac divisions remain unchanged. They are related directly to the seasons on Earth and historically to star constellations.

Each Sign of the Zodiac has specific meaning or effect. You probably know for example that Cancers tend to be feeling oriented and enjoy their home. But, to make profound accurate predictions, you need *not* know the *meaning* of the Signs. However, after completing this book, you should *continue* your study by learning the basics of the Signs.

Rather than having to write down the name of a Sign every time it is used, a symbol for each Sign was developed. The symbols are presented in Table #1. Just look them over. You are probably quite familiar with most of them. To the right of each symbol is a blank space where you can practice drawing. Or if you prefer, practice on a separate piece of paper. Either way, take some time to get familiar with the symbols by drawing them. There is no need to memorize them now. Later on you will be referring to the tables and by using them you will probably devote them to memory without trying.

Have you ever seen an illustration of our Solar system? When you look at all the Planets revolving around our Sun, you may have noticed that they do so on approximately the same plane. It looks sort of like they revolve around on a big plate. Roughly speaking, that plane is called the Ecliptic. If you draw twelve long lines on the plate using Earth as the center extending out into the Universe with each line representing a Sign (Taurus, Aries, Cancer, Pisces, etc.), you have drawn the Zodiac. That map would not fit on most desks, so

Table #1 - Zodiac Symbols

Sign	Symbol	Practice
Aries ---------	♈	
Taurus -------	♉	
Gemini ------	♊	
Cancer -------	♋	
Leo ----------	♌	
Virgo ---------	♍	
Libra ---------	♎	
Scorpio ------	♏	
Sagittarius ---	♐	
Capricorn ----	♑	
Aquarius -----	♒	
Pisces --------	♓	

Astrologers settle for a smaller one. Looking at Chart #1 (see page 11) you will see an example of the Zodiac Wheel. Did you notice that each Sign in the Zodiac is alloted exactly the same amount of space as the other Signs?

MEASUREMENT SYSTEM

The Zodiac serves as a map for plotting and viewing all the heavens that surround us. In order to pinpoint exact locations within the Zodiac, the geometric system for measuring angles is used. The first unite of measurement is the degree and the second is the minute. There are 360 degrees in a circle (the Zodiac) and 60 minutes in each degree.

Take another look at Chart #1. Notice that there are lines

dividing each Sign on the outside ring. There are 30 degrees in each Sign and there are twelve Signs. That gives the Zodiac exactly 360 degrees. *(Hint*: Degrees increase going counterclockwise in the Zodiac Wheel.)

When notating a location in the Zodiac, follow this procedure: First write the degrees, then the Sign, then the minutes. Below are some Zodiac notation examples. Look them over. Then, to gain more familiarity, do the Study Exercise which follows.

CHART #1 - The Zodiac

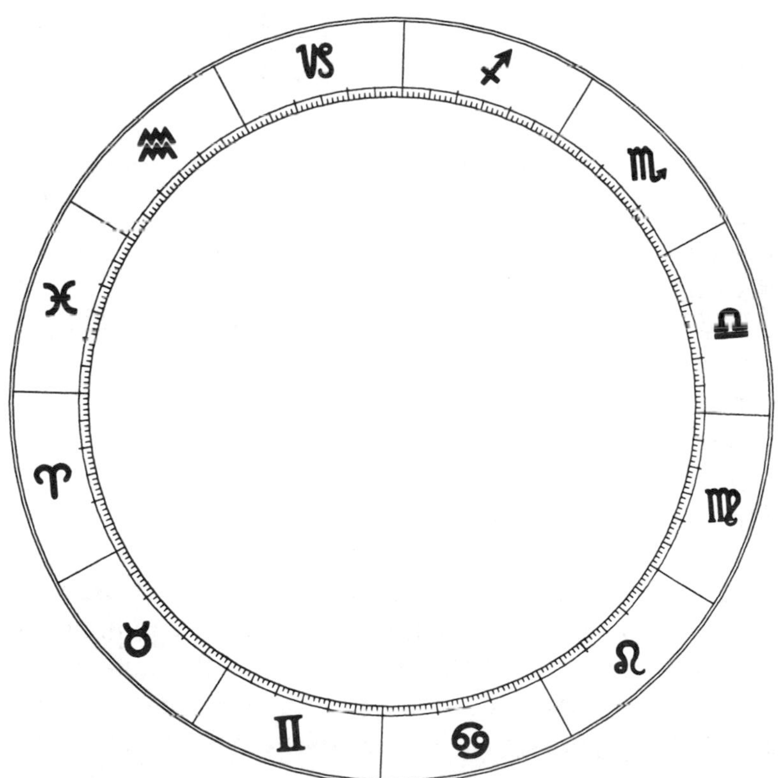

Zodiac Notation Examples

1) Five degrees twelve minutes in Taurus. 5°♉12′
2) Fourteen degrees one minute in Cancer. 14°♋1′
3) Five degrees ten minutes in Aries. 5°♈10′
4) Five degrees three minutes in Pisces. 5°♓3′
5) Twenty degrees two minutes in Gemini. 20°♊2′

STUDY EXERCISE - Zodiac Notation

Do this exercises to become more familiar with using the Astrological measurement system. Refer to Table #1 showing the symbols for the Signs. Write your answers in the space between each question. To check your work turn to Appendix four.

Step #1
Five degrees fifty-seven minutes in Cancer.

Step #2
Twenty-five degrees thirty-seven minutes in Taurus.

Step #3
Twenty two degrees and twenty-seven minutes in Cancer.

Step #4
Twenty-two degrees and seventeen minutes in the Sign of Capricorn.

Step #5
Three degrees and one minute in the Sign of Libra.

Step #6
Zero degrees nineteen minutes Scorpio.

STUDY EXERCISE - Plotting Locations in the Zodiac

In this study exercise you are going to practice plotting locations in the Zodiac. Use the locations from the Study Exercise above. Find these locations in Chart #1 on page 11. Make an "x" at the approximate location. Next to the "x", note the exact location using Zodiac notation.(Answers in Appendix four.) (*Hints:* Degrees and minutes increase going counter-clockwise. Degrees are small but visible on the Zodiac Wheel. Minutes are too small to be seen. Thus, you can only estimate positions when marking them on the Zodiac Wheel. However, Zodiac notation always gives you the exact location.)

THE PLANETS

Traditionally, Astrologers have called our Sun and Moon a Planet. Of course the Sun and the Moon are not Planets. The Sun is actually a star and our Moon is a Moon. When talking about them together with the Planets, saying "The Sun, the Moon and the Planets" is a mouth full. Saying just "the Planets" is much easier and everybody knows what you are talking about.

There are ten Planets. Each Planet has its own symbol. (Their are *two* symbols for Pluto.) Look at Table #2. There is no need at this time to memorize all the symbols for the Planets. But, to gain familiarity, to the right of each symbol is a space to practice drawing them. Take some time now to practice.

When I first studied Astrology I associated each symbol with something that was familiar to me. This makes it easier to recall the symbols. For example, the symbol for Mercury always reminded me of an inverted thermometer and a thermometer is filled with mercury. The symbol for Neptune looks like a big fork. I could see Neptune, King of the Sea holding that fork. An association that is most meaningful to you personally will help to recall the symbol.

When you start doing your own predictions you will be referring to the tables. At that time you probability will memorize them by using them. However, any associations you make with the symbols now will help to speed things along.

Planet's Exclusive Power

Each Planet has a unique and special power unto itself. The Planets do not share their individual powers with each other. They own them exclusively.

Table #2 - Planet Symbols

Planet	Symbol	Pratice
Moon -------	☽	
Sun ----------	☉	
Mercury ----	☿	
Venus -------	♀	
Mars---------	♂	
Jupiter ------	♃	
Saturn ------	♄	
Uranus ------	♅	
Neptune ----	♆	
Pluto --------	♇ or ♇	

The Manifester Planets

Your basic predictions will give you accurate, profound and important information. To do them, you need to know the powers of only two of the Planets: Jupiter and Saturn. Because these two Planets manifest many tangible changes, they are called the "Manifester Planets."

Read the sections below about the powers of the Manifester Planets for general understanding. To the right of each Planet is its "Essence Power." Remember the "Essence Power" for each Planet.

Saturn - Essence Power is Restriction

Volumes of information have been written about the specific powers of each Planet. The information has been written and compiled over a period of thousands of years. Everything I've read has given me more insight into the effects of each Planet. But, the essence power behind Saturn from which all else is derived lays in its ability to restrict. Through restricting, it causes a diversity of manifestations. But in essence, its only power is the power to restrict. As a point of illustration, marriage is a restriction. Marriage results when two people voluntarily create a restrictive and exclusive relationship between themselves. Saturn is the force behind all true marriages.

During its 29 year trip around the Zodiac, Saturn creates several predictable opportunities for committed relationships. Because of this predictability, it is also the clock behind marriage.

Jupiter - Essence Power is Expansion

Jupiter moves around the Zodiac about once every twelve years. So the cycles it creates are twelve-year cycles. Traditionally it has been considered the Planet of luck because it often brings very pleasant and abundant circumstances. But, in essence it has only the power to expand. From this, all of its manifestations occur. Examples are: expanded or increased income, expanded/excess love or "falling in love," buying a new home, expanding an existing home, having several marriage possibilities, etc.

THE HOUSES

Unlike Planets, the Houses are not physical things in the heavens. They are divisions of the Zodiac arrived at through mathematical calculations. These divisions are based on birth information and therefore unique to each individual's Birth Chart.

Look over Chart #2 which is Barbra Streisand's Birth Chart. Notice the lines dividing the circle. Each line is called a House Line. The space between two lines is a House. On the inside ring, the Houses are numbered 1 through 12.

Did you notice that the Zodiac divisions are not in the outer ring? Most often when House Lines are drawn in, the outer Zodiac ring is removed and the Zodiac Wheel is rotated. But, the exact points where the House Lines intersect the Zodiac are notated in the outside ring. That location of intersection of the House Line in the Zodiac is called the House Cusp.

There are many different methods used to calculate the House Lines. Each method has claims for its validity. The one recommended and used in this book is the Placidus system. I have found it to work well for prediction and is the most popular House system. If you used the forms in the back of the book to order your Charts, the Placidus House system will automatically be mailed to you. If you didn't order your Charts using the forms in the back of this book, make sure you asked for and are given the Placidus House system.

House Sign Rulership

The Sign that rules a House is the Sign intersected by its House Line. For example, look at Chart #2. Follow the 1st House Line to the outside ring where its position is notated as 6°♈38′. Thus, the 1st House Line intersects the Sign of Aries. Therefore, Aries rules the 1st House. (Note: If you didn't recognize the Sign symbol, turn to Table #1 on page 10.)

Let's do another example. What Sign Rules the 6th House? Following the 6th House Cusp Line to the outside ring, it shows that it is in the Sign of Leo. Therefore, Leo Rules the 6th House.

For more practice do the following Study Exercise.

CHART #2 -Natal Chart

Zodiac Signs	Pl	Planet	Plan's Sign	Hous	Position
♈ Aries	☽	Moon	Leo	5th	10° ♌ 34'
♉ Taurus	☉	Sun	Taurus	1st	03° ♉ 33'
♊ Gemini	☿	Mercury	Taurus	1st	08° ♉ 07'
♋ Cancer	♀	Venus	Pisces	12th	17° ♓ 34'
♌ Leo	♂	Mars	Gemini	3rd	28° ♊ 51'
♍ Virgo	♃	Jupiter	Gemini	3rd	19° ♊ 59'
♎ Libra	♄	Saturn	Taurus	2nd	28° ♉ 12'
♏ Scorpio	♅	Uranus	Taurus	2nd	28° ♉ 50'
♐ Sagittarius	♆	Neptune	Virgo	6th	27° ♍ 36' ℞
♑ Capricorn	♇	Pluto	Leo	5th	03° ♌ 29'
♒ Aquarius	☊	Node	Virgo	6th	10° ♍ 50'
♓ Pisces	Mc	Midheaven	Capricorn	10th	03° ♑ 31'
	Asc	Ascendant	Aries	1st	06° ♈ 38'

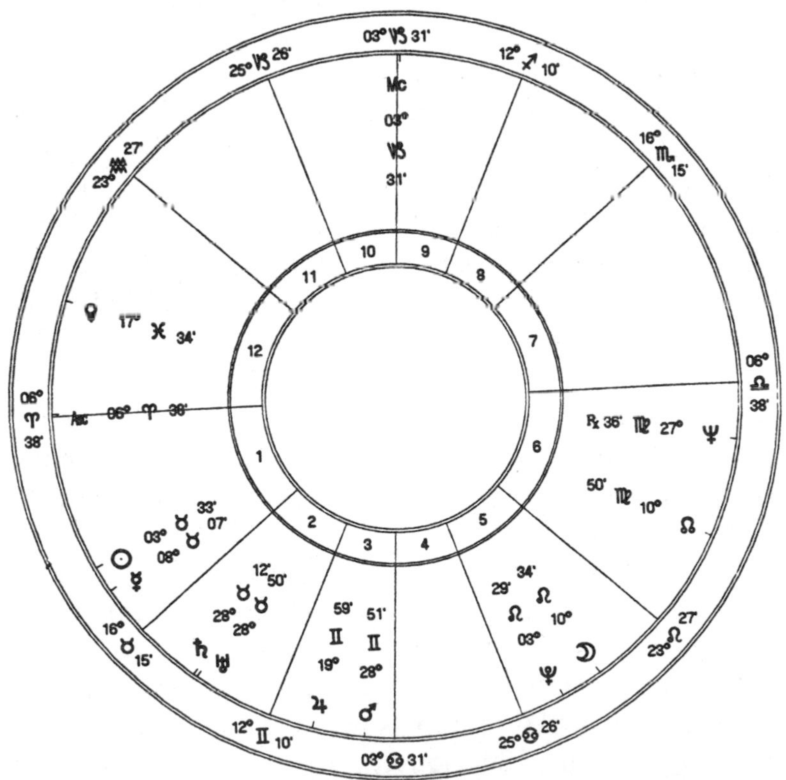

STUDY EXERCISE - House Sign Rulership

To determine House Sign Rulership, follow the House Line to the Sign it intersects. To check your work, turn to Appendix four.

Step #1

Find the Sign Ruling the 2nd House in Chart #2. (*Hint:* The House Line is the first line - going counterclockwise - within a specific House.)

Step #2

Write the Sign name and Sign symbol in the appropriate section in the Study Form below. (Note: For now, do not write in the far right column.)

Step #3

Follow Steps 1 and 2 above for all twelve Houses.

Co-Ruling Signs

A Co-Ruling Sign is a Sign that is contained completely within a House. For example, note the order of Signs going from the 12th House to the 1st House in Chart #2. Compare this to the natural order of Signs in the Zodiac in Chart #1. The Sign of Pisces is contained completely within the 12th House. Therefore, Pisces is the Co-Ruler of the 12th House.

Not all Charts have a Co-Ruling Sign. But, if there is one Co-Ruling Sign, there will always be another one which is located in the opposite House. For practice, using the method described in the above paragraph, determine the Co-Ruling Sign of the 6th House. (Note: The answer is located in the next paragraph.)

Keep track of Co-Ruling House Signs as you did the Ruling Signs. In the House Sign Rulership Study Form, just to the right of Leo in the 6th House Line, write "Virgo." Then, just to the right of the symbol for Leo in the 6th House Line, write in the symbol for Virgo. Now, enter the Co-Ruling Sign information for the 12th House.

STUDY FORM - House Sign Rulership

House	Ruling Sign	Symbol	
1st	____________	___	____________________
2nd	____________	___	____________________
3rd	____________	___	____________________
4th	____________	___	____________________
5th	____________	___	____________________
6th	____________	___	____________________
7th	____________	___	____________________
8th	____________	___	____________________
9th	____________	___	____________________
10th	____________	___	____________________
11th	____________	___	____________________
12th	____________	___	____________________

House Planet Rulership

Every Sign of the Zodiac is Ruled by a Planet. A Planet Rules a House by virtue of the House's Ruling Sign. Look over Table #3 on the next page. It shows all the Signs and to the right of each Sign is the Planet that Rules the Sign. Did you notice that some Planets Rule more than one Sign? There are twelve Signs and only ten Planets. Because of this, some of the Planets Rule more than one Sign.

There is no reason for you to memorize the table at this time. Later on you will be referring to it. As you use Table #3, you'll probably have it memorized without trying.

For practice finding House Planet Rulership, do the following Study Exercise.

STUDY EXERCISE - House Planet Rulership

Step #1

Determine the Planet that Rules and Co-Rules each House in the above Study Form by referring to Table #3.

Step #2

In the blank line to the far right in Study Form, write down the name and Symbol for each House Ruling and Co-Ruling Planet. To check you work turn to Appendix Four.

HOUSE POWERS

Each House Rules or governs a specific part of your life. For the prediction that you are going to, do you will be using four Houses.

Table #3 - Planet Rulership

Sign	Symbol	Ruling Planet	Symbol
Aries	♈	Mars	♂
Taurus	♉	Venus	♀
Gemini	♊	Mercury	☿
Cancer	♋	Moon	☽
Leo	♌	Sun	☉
Virgo	♍	Mercury	☿
Libra	♎	Venus	♀
Scorpio	♏	Pluto	♇/♇
Sagittarius	♐	Jupiter	♃
Capricorn	♑	Saturn	♄
Aquarius	♒	Uranus	♅
Pisces	♓	Neptune	♆

These are shown in Table #4 for easy reference. Keep in mind, these Houses govern many other issues in addition to the ones specifically shown here. These particular issues were selected because these are the matters you will be predicting. They got their nicknames ("House of Love," etc.) because they govern obviously important matters.

Once you have learned how to predict these major life concerns, you will be able expand your prediction into any area of your choosing by finding the House that Rules the matter of your concern.

Table #4 - House Rulership

House		Rules
2nd	———	House of Money
5th	———	House of Love
7th	———	House of Marriage
8th	———	House of Sexuality

THE NATAL CHART

When you were born, no doubt every one was very excited and happy. In the midst of the delight and cigars, someone probably wrote down the date, time and place of your birth. The birth information is called your Birth Data. (If you don't have your exact birth time, don't worry. Later on, I'll show you how to estimate it working backward.)

A Natal Chart shows the locations of all the Planet's Houses, etc., according to your Birth Data. (Natal: from Latin meaning "pertaining to one's birth.") The Natal Chart never changes because it is based specifically on permanent Birth Data.

Because of this, sometimes Astrologers refer to the Natal Chart as your Birth Chart or Birth Stamp.

Take another look at Chart #2 on page 17. It is the Natal Chart for Barbra Streisand. This is the same Chart you used in the House Sign Rulership Study Exercise. Notice that the approximate positions of the Planets are shown using their symbols and their exact locations are shown next to the Planet using Zodiac notation. Also, for easy reference, their locations are shown in a table on the same page.

THE EPHEMERIS

The Planets are continually moving in an orderly, predicatable manner. At any point in time, they are always somewhere. The locations of all the Planets are listed in a book called an Ephemeris. They are listed on a day-to-day basis according to their positions within the Zodiac. You will not need a complete Ephemeris now. In the back of this book I have included an abbreviated Ephemeris. It lists selected Planet locations on a biweekly basis. It contains all the information you need to make very profound and accurate predictions. Do the Study Exercise below using the Ephemeris provided in the back of the book (page 166). (Note: Answers are on page 164.)

STUDY EXERCISE - Using the Ephemeris

In this Study Exercise you are going to look up Planet positions from the Ephemeris in the back of the book. You will find the approximate location of each Planet on the date given.

a) Saturn on 7/7/96: Turn to the Ephemeris in the back of the book. Each block of numbers represents the Planet positions for one year. The year is located in the upper left hand corner of each block of numbers. Flip through the Ephemeris until you get to the year 1996. At the top of the block of numbers the Planet columns are listed. On the left of the block are the month rows. Follow the Saturn column down. As you follow the column down, each time the Planet moves into a new Sign, it is indicated with its respective symbol. For example, when you get to April 15th, you can see that Saturn goes into the Sign of Aries. The Planet's positions are shown for the 1st and the 15th of each month. So, when you get to July, you can estimate Saturn's position for the 7th, which is between the dates listed. But, for profound accurate predictions, all you really need is the Sign and the number of *degrees,* not the number of *minutes*. So, for 7/7/96 Saturn's position is approximately 7 degrees in the Sign of Aries. (Note: Sometimes the Planets appear to move backwards in the sky. Then the numbers will decrease instead of increase.)

b) Jupiter on 2/2/49
c) Neptune on 4/14/76
d) Pluto on 5/5/58
e) Jupiter on 8/8/94
f) Uranus on 5/1/98

ASPECTS

As the Planets move, they form angles to your Natal Planets and other locations in your Natal Chart. These angles are called Aspects. The Planets making the Aspects to the Natal Chart are called Transits. Thus, when referring to Planets there are two names: Natal Planets and Transiting Planets. Natal refers to their location in your Natal Chart and Transit refers to their new locations. Together they form angles which are called Aspects.

Each Aspect has a name, a symbol and has a specific effect. These are shown in Table #5. Look over the table and then read the section on the Powers of the Major Aspects below. Note that after each Aspect is a word that represents the *essence* of its power. Use this word as a keyword to recall the overall nature of the Aspect.

There is no need to memorize their powers now. When you start using the Aspects, you can refer to Table #5 and will be able to commit them to memory through use.

Powers of the Major Aspects

Through many years of study and observation by Astrologers the effects of Aspects have been quite well defined. There are only five Aspects discussed in this section. Astrologers have traditionally referred to them as the Major Aspects because they have the most profound effect on your life.

Before you read about them, keep in mind the following concept: Each Planet in your Natal Chart governs specific House issues such as love, income, etc. A Transiting Planet delivers power to those issues. The Aspect defines how the power is delivered. For example, the power of Transit Jupiter (excess) delivered thorough a Trine (harmony) would create excessive harmony. If this Aspect were being made to your 5th House of Love, the results would be conditions of excessive harmonious love. As you will find in the next chapter, many times people fall in love under this Aspect.

When you do your prediction, you will be able to go back in time in your life and see the profound effects of these Aspects. Meanwhile, remember the general function of Aspects: They determine how the power of a Transiting Planet is delivered.

Below is a general overview for each Major Aspect. While reading through them, refer to Chart #3 and Chart #4. They show the possible Aspect locations from a fixed point.

Conjunction - 0 Degrees - ☌ Essence is Unification

This position tends to unite the forces of the Transiting Planet with the Natal Planet in a positive, intensifying and synergistic manner. A distinct feature of the Conjunction is that it brings an ending prior to the new manifestation.

The overall conditions *allow* you personal control and/or intervention regarding the manifestation.

Sextiles - 60 Degrees - ⚹ Essence is Opportunity

This position creates favorable opportunity. The manifestation requires that you be aware of it and that you make an effort to bring about the manifestation. It is in that sence that it creates opportunity.

The overall conditions *require* personal control and/or intervention regarding the manifestation of the event to bring it about.

Square - 90 Degrees - □ Essence is Dissonance

When a Transiting Planet Squares the position of a Natal

Table #5 - Major Aspects

Aspect	Symbol	Degrees	Effect
Conjunction	☌	0	Unity
Sextiles	⚹	60	Opportunity
Square	□	90	Dissonance
Trine	△	120	Harmony
Opposition	☍	180	Opposition

Planet, its effect is dissonance, friction and/or disruption.

The overall conditions *demand* and allow personal control and/or intervention as well as inward processing regarding the manifestation of the event.

Trine - 120 Degree - △ Essence is Harmony

This position creates harmony. The manifestation is brought about in a harmonious manner and under harmonious conditions.

CHART #3
Zodiac Wheel Showing Major Aspects

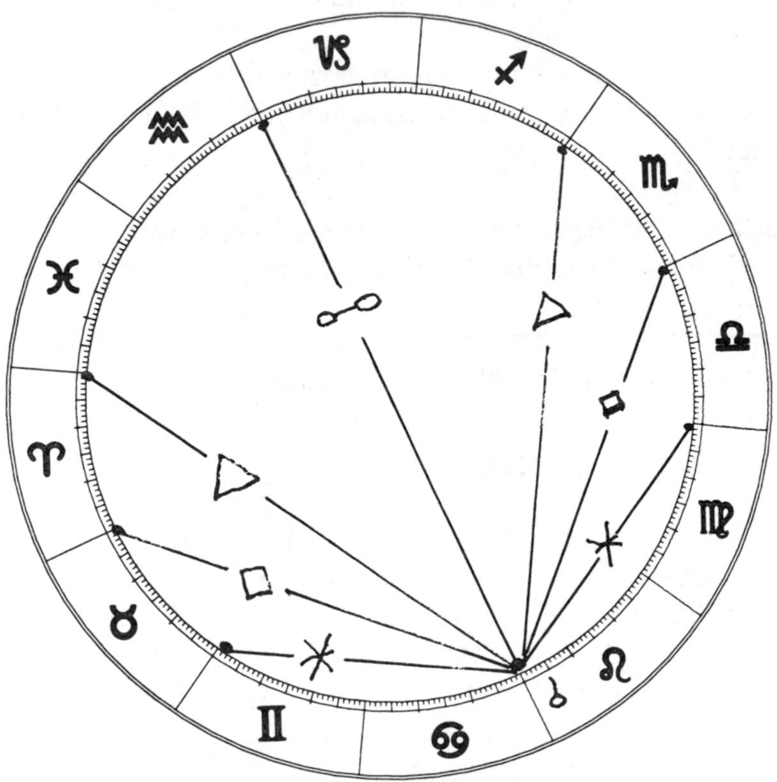

The overall conditions *allow* you personal control and/or intervention regarding the manifestation of the event.

Opposition - 180 Degrees - ☍ Essence is Opposition

When a Transiting Planet Opposes the position of a Natal Planet its effect is opposition. A distinct feature of the Opposition is that its manifestation is not a result of your efforts. It rests outside of your hands.

The overall conditions *do not allow* you personal control and/or intervention over the manifestation of the event.

CHART #4
Natal Chart Showing Major Aspects

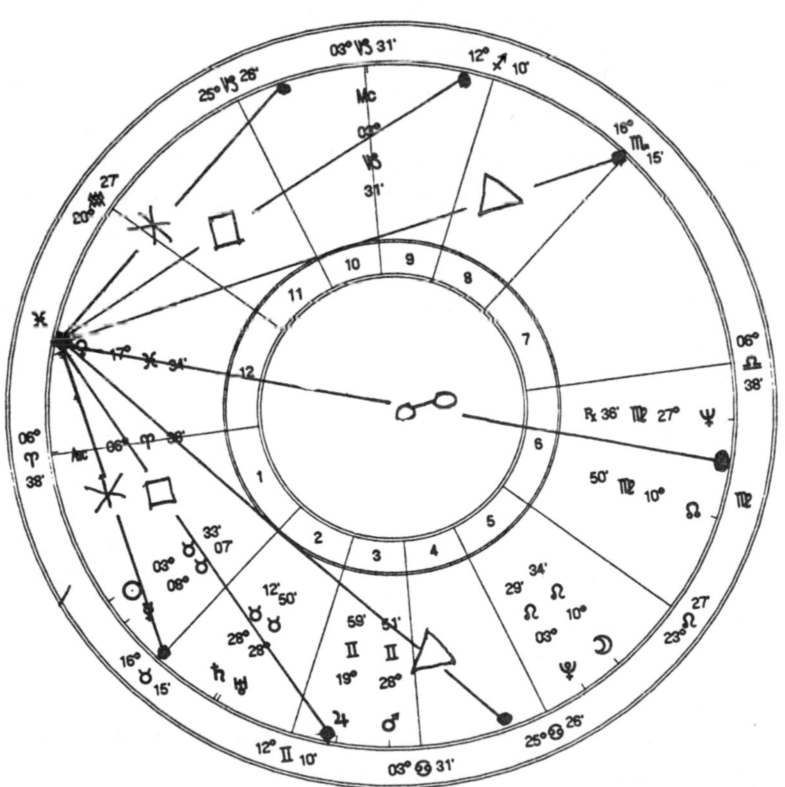

Hard and Soft Aspects

Did you notice that some Aspects bring harmonious conditions and others bring challenging conditions? For that reason, Astrologers have divided these Aspects into two groups: Hard Aspects/*challenge* and Soft Aspects/*harmony*. The Soft Aspects are: Conjunctions, Sextiles and Trines. The Hard Aspects are: Squares and Oppositions. Go back to Table #5 and next to each Aspect notate if it is a Hard Aspect or a Soft Aspect.

STUDY EXERCISE - Locating Aspects

In this exercise you are going to practice finding Aspects in Chart #5, which is a Zodiac Wheel.

Go through the exercise below marking the location for each Aspect using the appropriate Aspect symbol. Next to the Aspect write its exact location using Astrological notation.

To find Aspects, keep in mind that each Sign has exactly 30 degrees. To check your work, turn to Appendix Four.

Step #1

Using the appropriate symbol, mark the one possible location for an Opposition to 15 degrees Taurus. (*Hint:* Find 15° Taurus and go 180° in either direction. Each Sign is 30°.)

Step #2

Using the appropriate symbol, mark the two possible locations for Sextiles to 15 degrees Taurus. (*Hint:* From 15°♉, go 60° in both directions.)

Step #3

Using the appropriate symbol, mark the two possible locations for Squares to 15 degrees Taurus.

Step #4

Using the appropriate symbol, mark the two possible locations for Trines to 15 degrees Taurus.

Step #5

Using the appropriate symbol, mark the one possible location for a Conjunction to 15 degrees Taurus.

CHART #5
Study Exercise - Locating Aspects

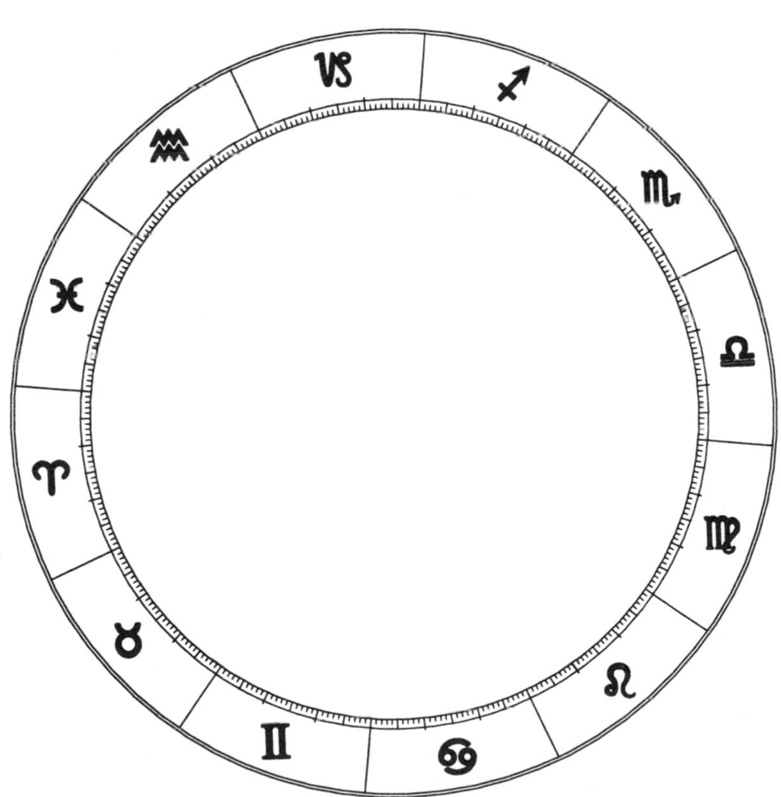

Chapter Two

PREDICTION

In this chapter you will be making your first predictions. I recommend that you study two Charts; yours and someone's you know. If you don't already have them, obtain them now. You'll be using these charts throughout the rest of the book. As a side note, make several identical copies of the charts you will be using. That way you can mark them up without having to buy a fresh chart every time you want a clean copy. Until you have your personal Charts in hand, you can continue this chapter by studying Barbra Streisand's Chart which is presented on page 17.

Because you will be simultaneously studying two Charts, for each Study Exercise in this chapter there are two Study Forms; one for your Chart and one for someone you know.

Take time now to go through Chapter One. Mark the pages containing Tables 3, 4 and 5. They are located on pages 20, 21 and 25. You will be referring to these throughout the book. By using them and making effort in the process, you probably will memorize them.

As a guideline for this chapter, keep the following principle in mind: Every House has a Ruling Planet. The Ruling Planet is sensitized to the House matters that it governs. In this chapter you will be studying how Transiting Saturn and Jupiter have affected your life by making Aspects to your 2nd, 5th, 7th and 8th House Ruling Planets. They govern respectively: money, love, commitment and sex.

HOUSE RULERSHIP

The first step in prediction is to determine the Ruling Planets for each House. Follow the Study Exercise below for your Chart and any other Chart you may be studying to determine House Rulership.

STUDY EXERCISE - House Rulership

In this section you are going to determine the Planets that Rule each of your Houses. The information will be placed into the Study Form below and referred to throughout this book. Then, the remainder of the sections in this chapter will give you a chance to start your first predictions.

The method used to determine House Rulership was explained in Chapter One. However, for this exercise, you will be guided one step at a time.

Step #1

Find the Sign in which your 1st House Cusp Line intersects the Zodiac. The Sign of intersection Rules your 1st House. Write the symbol of the Sign in the appropriate section in the Study Form below.

Step #2

Turn to Table #3 in Chapter One. Follow the Sign column down until you reach the Ruling Sign of your 1st House. To the right of the Sign is the Planet that Rules that Sign. That Planet Rules your 1st House. Write the symbol of the Planet in the appropriate section in the Study Form below.

Repeat steps 1 and 2 for all twelve Houses.

Step #3

In this step you are going to determine if your 1st House has a Co-Ruling Sign and Planet. *(Hint:* A Co-Ruling Sign is a Sign that is contained completely within a House.*)*

Noting the Ruling Signs of your 1st and 2nd Houses, look at the Zodiac Wheel on page 11. If the Zodiac Wheel shows that there is a Sign between your 1st House and 2nd House Signs, then that Sign is contained completely within your 1st House. It is the Co-Ruling Sign of your 1st House. Write the symbol of the Co-Ruling Sign next to the Ruling Sign in your Study Form.

Now, follow Step #2 above to determine the Planet that Rules the Co-Ruling Sign of your 1st House. That Planet is the Co-Ruling Planet of your 1st House. Write its symbol next to the Ruling Planet in your Study Form. Repeat this step checking each House for Co-Ruling Signs.

Step #4

Locate the position of the Planet in your Natal Chart that Rules (and Co-Rules if applicable) your 1st House. Copy its location into the appropriate section below.

Note: The Planets' approximate positions are shown in your Natal Chart by using the symbol of the Planet placed in the Chart. The exact location of the Planet, using Astrological notation, is shown in the Planet list on your Chart and/or next to the Planet symbol.

Repeat this step for each of your Houses.

STUDY FORM - House Rulership

House	Ruling Sign	Ruling Planet	Location
1st	________	________	____________
2nd	________	________	____________
3rd	________	________	____________
4th	________	________	____________
5th	________	________	____________
6th	________	________	____________
7th	________	________	____________
8th	________	________	____________
9th	________	________	____________
10th	________	________	____________
11th	________	________	____________
12th	________	________	____________

7TH HOUSE SATURN CYCLE

The 7th House governs all one-on-one relationships. Most often marriage occurs when Transit Saturn makes a Soft Aspect (Conjunction, Sextile or Trine) to the 7th House Ruling Planet on the Natal Chart. This happens because Transit Saturn has the power to restrict. When this restriction is delivered to the 7th House Ruling Planet via a Soft Aspect, conditions for commitment become natural, comfortable, harmonious, personally beneficial and/or desirable. Depending on the age, maturity, marital status, history and desires of the

STUDY FORM - House Rulership

House	Ruling Sign	Ruling Planet	Location
1st	________	________	____________
2nd	________	________	____________
3rd	________	________	____________
4th	________	________	____________
5th	________	________	____________
6th	________	________	____________
7th	________	________	____________
8th	________	________	____________
9th	________	________	____________
10th	________	________	____________
11th	________	________	____________
12th	________	________	____________

subject, this can be translated into making a best friend, going steady, a positive period of marriage or getting married itself. If Saturn's power is delivered through a Hard Aspect (Square or Opposition) committed relationships are challenged. When divorce does occurs, it is usually under a Hard Saturn Aspect. If divorce does not occur under this Aspect, the relationship is strengthened due to the challenges the Aspect brings forward.

Saturn revolves around the Zodiac about once every 29 years. During the cycle it makes five Soft and three Hard Aspects to the 7th House Ruling Planet. The cycle is called the 7th House Saturn cycle and accurately defines the ongoing conditions of marriage.

Before we go further, I want to mention something in order to prepare you for more advanced prediction methods. Although Transit Saturn's relationship to the 7th House Ruling Planet is the key to predicting marriage and divorce, there are nine other Transits. Each has profound effect on 7th House conditions. They do not however cause beginnings and endings as does Transit Saturn. Transit Saturn can always be used to predict marriage.

Rather than just reading about this, using your own Chart, you are now going to study how it has worked in your life. The general guideline is: Soft Aspects create committed relationships and Hard Aspects challenge them.

This 7th House Saturn Cycle study is always the beginning step in prediction. The first time you do it, it may seem a bit tedious. But, after you go through it one time it becomes very easy.

STUDY EXERCISE - 7th House Saturn Cycle

Below are the five steps for determining your 7th House Saturn Cycle. If you get stuck, go back to Chapter One and review the particular area that is not clear to you.

Step #1

Using your House Rulership Study Form, copy the 7th House Ruling Sign, Ruling Planet and Planet location into the appropriate Study Form section on the next page. If you have a 7th House Co-Ruling Planet, include it in each step.

Step #2

Using the Zodiac Wheel provided on the next page as a guide, locate all the Major Aspects (see Table #5) to the Ruling Planet of your 7th House. Write these locations onto the Zodiac Wheel notating the kind of Aspect and its location. These notes will serve as a permanent reference for studying your Chart. (*Hint:* Mark the position of your 7th House Ruling Planet on the Zodiac Wheel, then find the Aspects.)

(Note: If you ordered "The Works" from the back of the book, this information has been looked up for you. Skip to Step #3 below.)

Step #3

Find the month and year when Transiting Saturn makes/made these Aspects.

Using the Ephemeris in the back of the book, locate the month and year when Saturn makes the Aspects found in Step #2 above. Enter this information in the appropriate sections in the Study Form below. For a starting date, use the year when you were about ten years old. For an ending date, add about five years from today.

An easy way to use the Ephemeris, is by keeping one finger on the Zodiac while the other hand goes through the Ephemeris. Take your time. There are a lot of dates to look up. This is an important record that will serve as a personal reference tool for all your studies.

(Note: If you ordered "The Works," these dates are already indexed. Transiting Planets are on the far left, then there is a line leading to the Aspect. Right next to the Aspect symbol is the Natal Planet being Aspected on your Chart and the date.)

Step #4

In this step, you are going to go back in time and make notes about past committed relationships. Enter the date they began and the date they ended. Write this next to an Aspect which is close to the time of the event. Then make a brief comment. For example: '60 first boyfriend, 4/67 married Tom, '71 divorced Tom, 10/72 met Fred, 3/73 moved in with Fred,

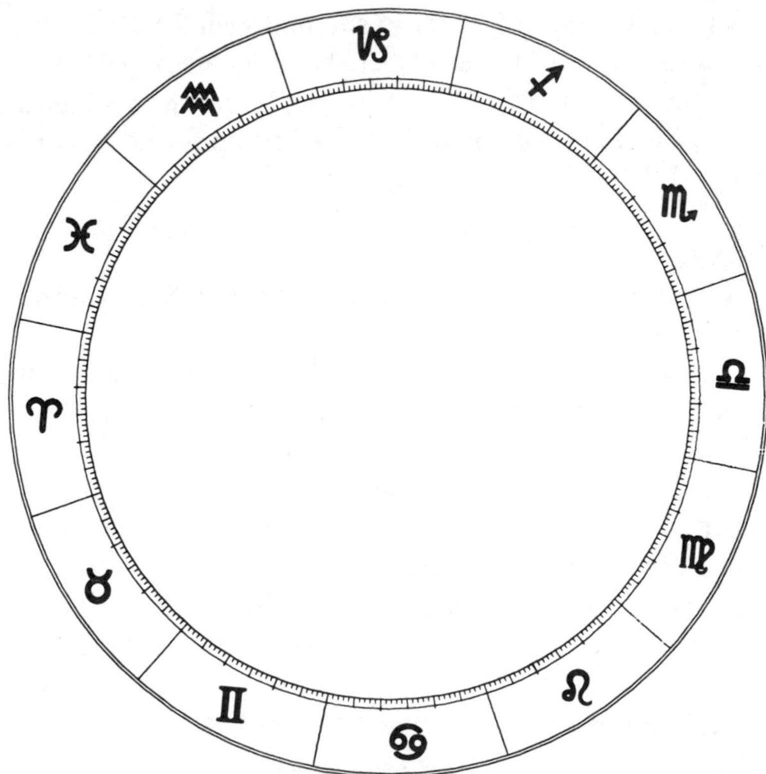

STUDY FORM - 7th House Saturn Cycle

Ruling Sign	Ruling Planet	Location
___________	_____________	_________

Month/Year	Aspect	Comment
____________	_________	
____________	_________	
____________	_________	
____________	_________	
____________	_________	
____________	_________	
____________	_________	
____________	_________	
____________	_________	
____________	_________	
____________	_________	
____________	_________	
____________	_________	
____________	_________	
____________	_________	
____________	_________	
____________	_________	
____________	_________	
____________	_________	
____________	_________	
____________	_________	
____________	_________	
____________	_________	
____________	_________	
____________	_________	

STUDY FORM - 7th House Saturn Cycle

Ruling Sign	Ruling Planet	Location
____________	____________	____________

Month/Year	Aspect	Comment
____________	________	
____________	________	
____________	________	
____________	________	
____________	________	
____________	________	
____________	________	
____________	________	
____________	________	
____________	________	
____________	________	
____________	________	
____________	________	
____________	________	
____________	________	
____________	________	
____________	________	
____________	________	
____________	________	
____________	________	
____________	________	
____________	________	
____________	________	
____________	________	
____________	________	

'75 moved out, '79 committed to Mark, etc. Depending upon your age, a professional Astrologer would expect to see no more that about five or six comments.

Predicting - Marriage/Commitment

Now that you have all the detailed work finished, look over your 7th House Saturn Cycle for overall basic trends. If you have a Co-Ruling Planet, then you have to take both Planets into consideration. The general trend you should find is that commitments were made under Soft Aspects and challenged or ended during Hard Aspects. Sometimes this will appear dramatically in a Chart and sometimes the dates may seem off. You may even find events that don't actually connect at all with your Saturn Cycle. This is normal. Later you can go back to each major 7th House event using advanced studies to see exactly what was going on. But for now, you are looking for general trends created by Transit Saturn.

If the trends seem to follow the Aspects then you are ready to make your first basic prediction. Simply note the next Aspect made by Saturn to your 7th House Ruling Planet. This will tell you the forthcoming condition in your life regarding committed relationships. Soft Aspects create commitments and Hard Aspects challenge them.

(Note: If for some reason, none of the trends seem to match, double check your work. If the problem is still not resolved you probably do not have the correct 7th House Ruling Planet. In that case, you can work backwards by looking up the dates in the Ephemeris in which you made or ended major commitments. Then note what Natal Planet Transiting Saturn was Aspecting on those dates. If that does not rectify the problem, you are going to need more advanced skills to correct the difficulty. Don't get discouraged. Try studying a friend's Chart until you understand the difficulty with your own.)

LOVE

Who you love and who loves you is governed entirely by the 5th House of Love. For this exercise, you are going to study the one year periods around the times you "fell in love." I recommend that you use your 7th House Saturn Cycle to find a period in which you "fell in love" plus made a commitment.

The essence of all Jupiter's effects come from its power to expand. It takes twelve years for it to make a complete cycle around the Zodiac. People most often fall in love when Jupiter's power of expansion is delivered through a Soft Aspect to the 5th House Ruling Planet. Thus, you will be studying Jupiter's relationship to your 5th House Ruling Planet first, then you will study Transit Saturn.

STUDY EXERCISE - Love

Once you have had a chance to study your past love conditions in this Study Exercise, you will continue by studying the future conditions and then make predictions.

<u>Step #1</u>

Using your House Rulership Study Form, copy the data concerning your 5th House into the appropriate sections in the Study Form below. If you have Co-Ruling Planet, include it in each step.

<u>Step #2</u>

Using the Zodiac provided, notate the position of all Aspects that can be made to your 5th House Ruling Planets. (Note: If you ordered "The Works," this information has already been looked up for you. Skip to Step #3.)

Step #3

a) Starting about one year before and containing one year after you "fell in love," look up dates using the Ephemeris in the back of the book when Aspects were made by Transit Jupiter to your 5th House Ruling Planet. Notate the month and year in the appropriate place in the Study Form below. Leave a blank line for every line you use. Later, you will be using the blank line for Saturn Aspects.

If you ordered "The Works," this information has already been looked up for you. Simply follow the column on the left until you find an Aspect made by Jupiter to your 5th House Ruler.

b) Follow step "a" above, starting about one year ago and continue through the next 3 years.

Step #4

Using the Comment section in the Study Form, note any issues you recall about falling in love including the month and year.

Step #5

Review the Comment section for the general trends as they relate to the Aspects. There should be Soft Aspects around the time you fell in love and Hard Aspects around the time your love relationships were challenged. If the exact pattern does not follow, later when you begin more advanced methods, you can go back in time and study this again.

If the Comment section follows the general pattern of the Aspects, then make predictions based on the forthcoming Aspects. Follow the guideline: Soft Aspects are harmonious and Hard Aspects are challenging.

STUDY FORM - Love

House	Ruling Sign	Ruling Planet	Location
5th	________	________	____________

Month/Year	Aspect	Comment
__________	_______	
__________	_______	
__________	_______	
__________	_______	
__________	_______	
__________	_______	
__________	_______	
__________	_______	
__________	_______	
__________	_______	
__________	_______	
__________	_______	
__________	_______	
__________	_______	

Predicting - Love Using Jupiter and Saturn

Jupiter has the power to expand and Saturn has the power to restrict. As you found in this exercise, conditions for falling in love are created when Jupiter's power of expansion is delivered through a Soft Aspect. But, Saturn often plays a very important and key role in the love scenario as well. Because Saturn has the power to restrict, under a Soft Aspect to the

Ruler of your 5th House of Love, this can result in restricting your love to one person. On the other hand, a Soft Aspect delivered by Jupiter and a Hard Aspects delivered by Saturn can create mixed conditions where falling in love comes easy but restricting this love to one person becomes stressful. The general condition of 5th House issues can *always* be determined by Transiting Jupiter and Saturn.

Follow Steps #1 to #5 above, but this time use Transit *Saturn.* Try to maintain the chronological order of Aspects by using the lines you left blank.

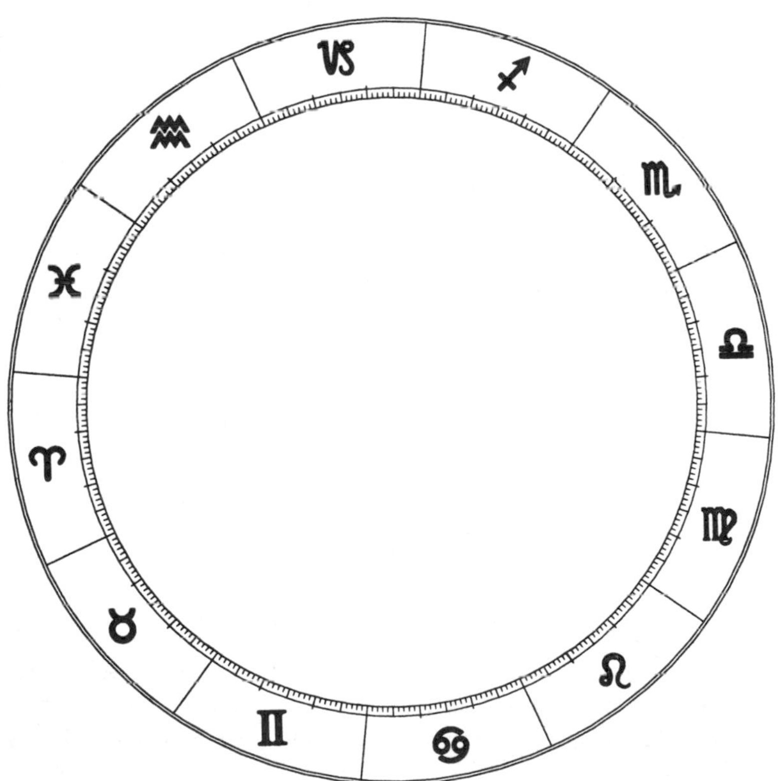

STUDY FORM - Love

House	Ruling Sign	Ruling Planet	Location
5th	________	________	____________

Month/Year	Aspect	Comment
__________	_______	
__________	_______	
__________	_______	
__________	_______	
__________	_______	
__________	_______	
__________	_______	
__________	_______	
__________	_______	
__________	_______	
__________	_______	
__________	_______	
__________	_______	
__________	_______	

SEX

Sexuality is governed by the 8th House. One of the best ways to begin studying this House is to go back in time to the year that you "lost your virginity," Study the dates Transiting Jupiter and Saturn were making Aspects to your 8th House Ruler.

Once you have had a chance to study this time period, you will proceed to examine a *commitment* date from your 7th House Saturn Cycle. Then study your future 8th House Aspects and make predictions.

STUDY EXERCISE - Sex

<u>Step #1</u>

Using your House Rulership Study Form, copy the data concerning your 8th House into the appropriate sections in the Study Form on the next page. If you have an 8th House Co-Ruling Planet, include it in each step.

<u>Step #2</u>

Using the Zodiac provided, note the position of all Aspects that can be made to your 8th House Ruling Planet. (Note: If you ordered "The Works" this information has already been looked up for you. Skip to Step #3.)

<u>Step #3</u>

Step #3 is divided into three sections: the time when you "lost you virginity," the time when you made a commitment and the future. Also, in this Study Exercise you will be following two Planets in the Emphemeris at the same time; Jupiter and Saturn.

a) Start about one year before and continue one year after you "lost your virginity." Using the Ephemeris in the back of the book, look up the month and year when Aspects were made by Jupiter and Saturn to your 8th House Ruling Planet. Notate these in the appropriate place in the Study Form.

b) Now look up Aspects made by Jupiter and Saturn a year

before to a year after you made a commitment.

c) Finally, look up Aspects starting about one year ago and continuing for about two years.

(Note: If you ordered "The Works," this information has already been looked up for you.)

Step #4

For past Aspects, notate any sexual involvement you recall in the Comment section of your Study Form.

STUDY FORM - Sex

House	Ruling Sign	Ruling Planet	Location
8th	________	________	____________

Month/Year	Aspect	Comment
____________	________	
____________	________	
____________	________	
____________	________	
____________	________	
____________	________	
____________	________	
____________	________	
____________	________	
____________	________	
____________	________	
____________	________	
____________	________	

Predicting - Sex

Review the Comment section for the general trends as they relate to the Aspects. There should be Soft Aspects around the time you "lost your virginity." If the exact pattern does not follow, later when you begin more advanced methods, you can go back in time and study this again. If the Comment section follows the general pattern of the Aspects, then make predictions based on your forthcoming Aspects.

STUDY FORM - Sex

House	Ruling Sign	Ruling Planet	Location
8th	________	________	____________

Month/Year	Aspect	Comment
__________	_______	
__________	_______	
__________	_______	
__________	_______	
__________	_______	
__________	_______	
__________	_______	
__________	_______	
__________	_______	
__________	_______	
__________	_______	
__________	_______	
__________	_______	

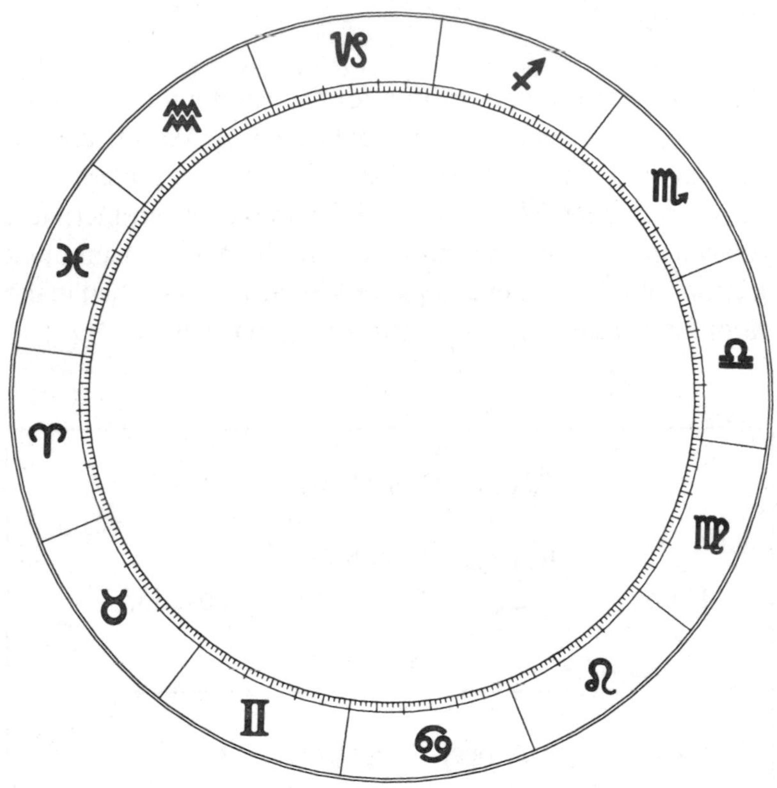

MONEY

Money is Ruled by two Houses; the 2nd House and the 8th House. The 2nd House deals primarily with disposable cash. Disposable cash is money that you have readily available to spend. The 8th House governs shared assets which include such things as taxes, loans and assets that are shared in a marriage. As you found in the previous Study Exercise, the 8th House also governs sexuality. However, in this section you will be focusing on shared assets.

When studying money, the Transits to examine are the Manifester Planets: Jupiter and Saturn. Jupiter is the Planet of expansion and Saturn is the Planet of restriction. The way in which Transit Jupiter and Saturn are Aspected to the Rulers of your 8th and 2nd House determine your overall financial situation. Soft Aspects tend to be beneficial and Hard Aspects tend to be challenging. Because you are examining two Houses and two Transits, things become more complex.

Take time now to study your own financial cycles by doing the study exercise below.

STUDY EXERCISE - Money

Step #1

Using your House Rulership Study Exercise, copy the 2nd and 8th House Rulership information into the appropriate sections below. If you have Co-Ruling Planet, include them in each step.

Step #2

Using the Zodiac provided, note the position of all Aspects that can be made to your 8th and 2nd House Ruling Planets. (Note: If you ordered "The Works," this information has already been looked up for you.)

Step #3

Recalling income periods is sometimes easy and sometimes difficult. If you can recall a specific period in time in which you had a dramatic shift in income, study this period then focus on the future. If not, start about three years ago and continue about three years into the future.

Using the Ephemeris in the back of the book, determine the month and year Aspects were made by both Transiting Jupiter and Transiting Saturn to both your 8th and 2nd House

Ruling Planets for these time periods. (Note: If you ordered "The Works," this information has already been looked up for you.)

Step #4

Notate any financial situations you recall in the Comment section of your Study Form.

Step #5

Review the Comment section to see if financial trends fol-

STUDY FORM - Money

House	Ruling Sign	Ruling Planet	Location
2nd	________	________	____________
8th	________	________	____________

Month/Year	Aspect	Comment
________	________	
________	________	
________	________	
________	________	
________	________	
________	________	
________	________	
________	________	
________	________	
________	________	
________	________	
________	________	
________	________	

lowed the Aspects. The Soft Aspects should show an increase in income and Hard Aspects should show income challenges.

Step #6

If the Comment section follows the general pattern of the Aspects then you can make predictions based on the forthcoming Aspects.

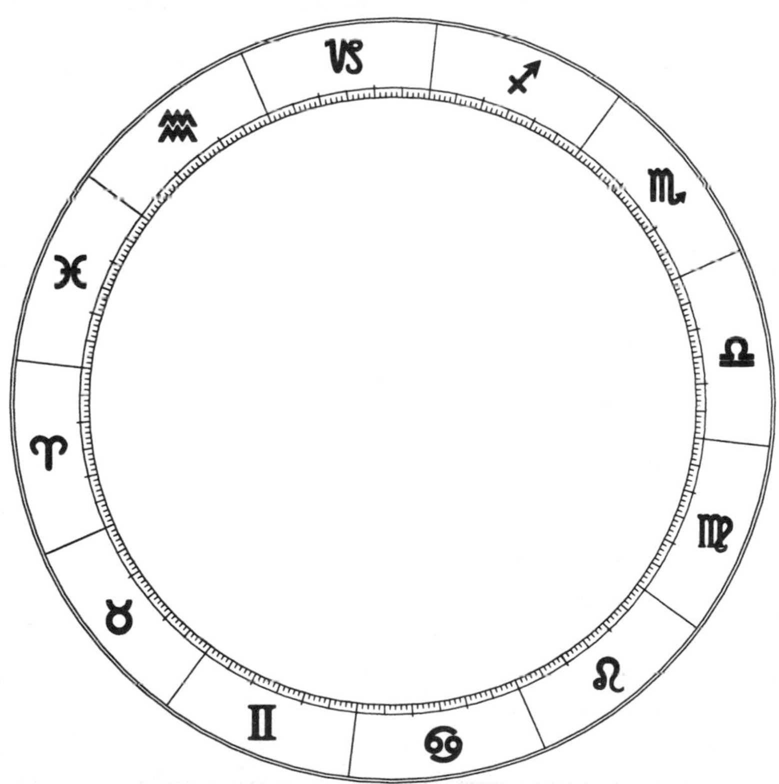

Predicting - Money/Income

This is the guideline to follow once you have determined that you can predict your income cycles: Save during high income cycles. If you have saved during high income periods, then you are covered during the challenging Hard Aspects.

A high income Jupiter Cycle can be tricky. Along with the income, Jupiter creates the feeling that it will go on forever. But, it doesn't. It just makes you feel that way. The feeling is

STUDY FORM - Money

House	Ruling Sign	Ruling Planet	Location
2nd	________	________	________
8th	________	________	________

Month/Year	Aspect	Comment
________	________	
________	________	
________	________	
________	________	
________	________	
________	________	
________	________	
________	________	
________	________	
________	________	
________	________	
________	________	
________	________	
________	________	

part of the effects of Jupiter. So, even though you may feel like money will keep rolling in the door for eternity, *save.*

The best way to deal emotionally with the Hard Jupiter and Saturn Aspects is to simply realize that you will have to work a little harder for the same amount of money. Allow yourself to have patience during these periods and try to save before they arrive. Also, it is an excellent time to lay foundation for high income periods.

The lasting effects of the Soft Jupiter and Saturn Aspects often are associated with moving into a higher income bracket. For example, Soft Aspects may indicate a raise.

The Soft Aspects made by Transiting Saturn are usually very practical in terms of saving. Saturn's power is one of restriction and a Soft Aspect usually means that the restriction is desirable. For example, you may have an increase in income during a Saturn Trine to the Ruler of your 2nd House. But, rather than having the desire to expand (the Jupiter feeling) your life by spending it as it comes in the door, you may desire to save all of it to buy a house. Thus, the money is there but it is restricted.

Unlike predicting marriage, which focused on the event date, the income predictions focus on the overall cycles. For example if you note that Transiting Jupiter is one year away from Conjuncting the Ruler of your 2nd House, that one year period of time prior to the Aspect becoming Exact would be indicative of a high income period. This is a time when all your efforts to bring in income are blessed. The income increase should be noticeable when the Aspect comes within ten degrees of becoming Exact. Plus, on about the date the Aspect becomes Exact, you should be able to predict a lump some of money.

As an interesting side note, a Soft Aspect made to the 8th House Ruler by Jupiter is often associated with finding money in the street. Somewhere out there is a shared asset pool of funds that we all have contributed to when money falls out of our pocket. It is during this Aspect that we receive from it.

As you study your income cycles keep in mind that you are studying four cycles. Each House (2nd and 8th) has two cycles: a Saturn Cycle and a Jupiter Cycle. They intermingle and operate at the same time. This can become even more complex if you are working with a Co-Ruling Planet.

FREE STUDY

The following Free Study Exercise will give you a chance to examine any part of your life which you desire.

To determine the House you wish to investigate, look over Appendix Two. I strongly suggest that you first study a House issue that has some tangible form in your life; for example the 10th House of Career.

STUDY EXERCISES - Free Study

Step #1

Turn to the Appendix Two (see page 151) in the back the book. Look through the various Houses until you find one that you would like to study.

Step #2

Using your House Rulership Study Form, copy pertinent House Rulership information into the appropriate sections in this Study Form. Study any Co-Ruling Planet you may have along with the Ruling Planet.

Step #3

Using the Zodiac Chart provided, mark the location for all Aspects made to the Ruling Planet under study. (Note: If you purchased "The Works," this information has already been indexed for you.)

<u>Step #4</u>

In this step you have to decide the time periods in the past that you want to study. Focus on times when there were notable changes regarding the House issues. Then study a period of time starting now and going an appropriate amount of time into the future.

Using the Ephemeris in the back of the book, look up the dates that Aspects were made by both Transiting Saturn and Jupiter to the Planet under study for the time periods you selected. Or, simply transcribe this data from "The Works."

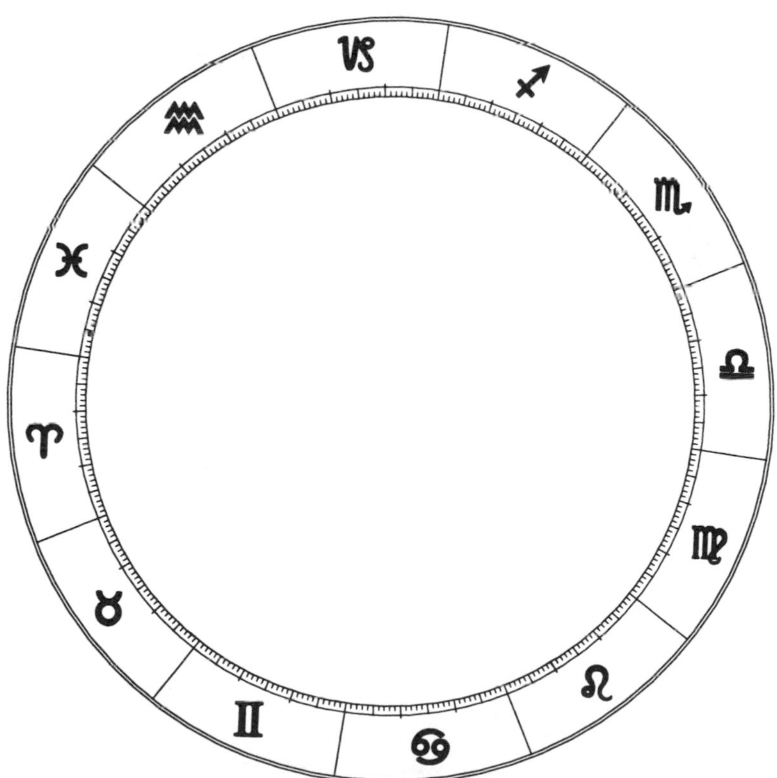

Step #5

Notate changes you recall regarding House issues in the Comment section.

Prediction - Free Study

Review the Comment section for basic trends. If the trends seem to follow the Aspects, then predict future conditions based on future Aspects. (Note: Several extra forms and two Zodiac Wheels are provided for this study.)

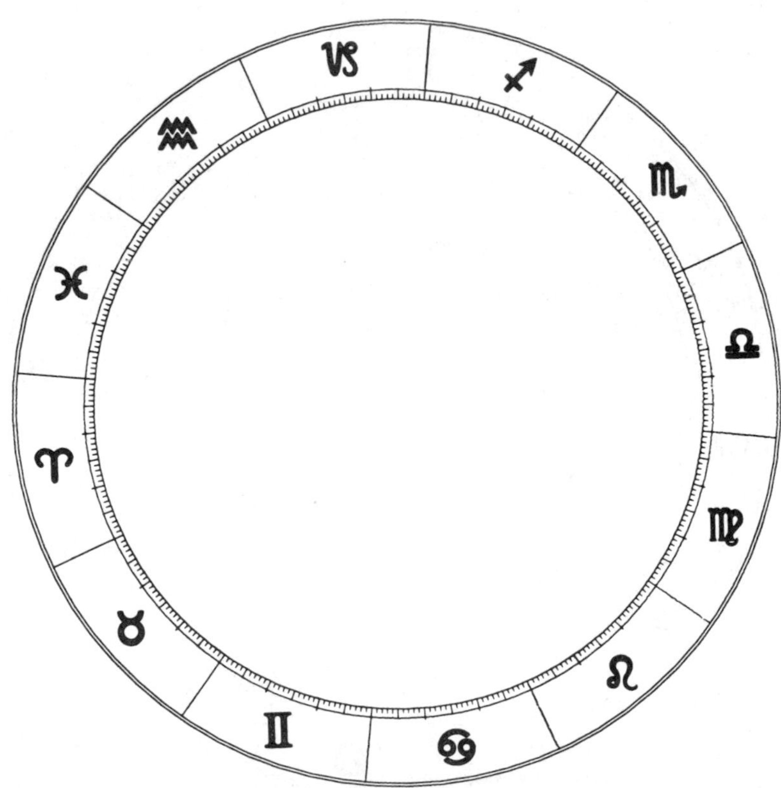

STUDY FORM - Free Study

House	Ruling Sign	Ruling Planet	Location
____	____________	____________	________

Month/Year	Aspect	Comment
____________	________	
____________	________	
____________	________	
____________	________	
____________	________	
____________	________	
____________	________	
____________	________	
____________	________	
____________	________	
____________	________	
____________	________	
____________	________	
____________	________	
____________	________	
____________	________	
____________	________	
____________	________	
____________	________	
____________	________	
____________	________	
____________	________	
____________	________	
____________	________	
____________	________	
____________	________	

STUDY FORM - Free Study

House	Ruling Sign	Ruling Planet	Location
____	__________	__________	________

Month/Year	Aspect	Comment
__________	________	
__________	________	
__________	________	
__________	________	
__________	________	
__________	________	
__________	________	
__________	________	
__________	________	
__________	________	
__________	________	
__________	________	
__________	________	
__________	________	
__________	________	
__________	________	
__________	________	
__________	________	
__________	________	
__________	________	
__________	________	
__________	________	
__________	________	
__________	________	
__________	________	
__________	________	

STUDY FORM - Free Study

House	Ruling Sign	Ruling Planet	Location
____	____________	____________	_________

Month/Year	Aspect	Comment
____________	_________	
____________	_________	
____________	_________	
____________	_________	
____________	_________	
____________	_________	
____________	_________	
____________	_________	
____________	_________	
____________	_________	
____________	_________	
____________	_________	
____________	_________	
____________	_________	
____________	_________	
____________	_________	
____________	_________	
____________	_________	
____________	_________	
____________	_________	
____________	_________	
____________	_________	
____________	_________	
____________	_________	
____________	_________	
____________	_________	

STUDY FORM - Free Study

House	Ruling Sign	Ruling Planet	Location
_____	__________	__________	________

Month/Year	Aspect	Comment
____________	________	
____________	________	
____________	________	
____________	________	
____________	________	
____________	________	
____________	________	
____________	________	
____________	________	
____________	________	
____________	________	
____________	________	
____________	________	
____________	________	
____________	________	
____________	________	
____________	________	
____________	________	
____________	________	
____________	________	
____________	________	
____________	________	
____________	________	
____________	________	
____________	________	
____________	________	

Chapter Three

ADVANCED PREDICTION

This chapter offers several real life examples many of which are contained within "The Professor" on the following page. In addition, specific advanced Predictive Astrological techniques are considered. Each section will give you additional skills for refining your predictions.

Take your time with this chapter. This chapter, Chapter Four, the case study in Chapter Five, and the Appendices can be used as references throughout your Astrological studies. In addition, they should lead you to your own discoveries and need for additional supportive Astrological texts.

If you know the subject you are studying, you can accurately predict commitment simply by using Transit Saturn's relationship to the 7th House Ruling Planet. But, this should only be the starting point for predicting marriage. The entire Marriage Scenario includes falling in love, sexuality and making a commitment. These are respectively 5th, 8th and 7th House matters. To predict marriage, study the Ruling Planets of theses Houses in relationship to the Manifester Planets; Transiting Jupiter and Saturn.

"The Professor" example below will illustrates the Ideal Marriage Scenario. By reading it, you have your first opportunity to read Astrological text. Take your time and follow the examples using his Chart.

THE PROFESSOR

Chart #6 belongs to a friend of mine. He's a professor of Music at Berkeley. He is also an accomplished performer who tours playing his New Age piano compositions. We met in Maui in 1992 when he was returning from a world tour. At the time, he was camping at the Seven Sacred Pools enjoying the freedom of his bachelor life.

In February of the following year, I pulled up his Chart on my computer. It strongly indicated that in about one week he was going to fall in love and propose marriage. The striking part of this was that I predicted it would all occur on about the same day. This scenario is quite different from falling in love in month one and proposing six months down the road.

At the time I made the marriage prediction I did not know if the Professor had a lady friend. He had spent almost the

CHART #6
The Professor's Natal Chart

The Professor
AUG 21 1953 Trop

☉	28°♌04'	-0°00'
☽	11°♑47'	-1°55'
☿	12°♌16'	+0°42'
♀	19°♋55'	-0°56'
♂	14°♌33'	+1°00'
♃	21°♊58'	-0°35'
♄	23°♎14'	+2°21'
♅	21°♋08'	+0°26'
♆	21°♎45'	+1°39'
♇	23°♌05'	+9°20'
☊	01°♒46'	-0°00'
Mc	29°♉05'	-0°00'
As	04°♍14'	-0°00'

Feb 01 1993

☉	13°♒08'	-0°00'
☽	06°♊39'	+1°12'
☿	19°♒51'	-1°53'
♀	29°♓31'	+1°26'
♂℞	09°♋49'	+3°57'
♃℞	14°♎40'	+1°27'
♄	20°♒00'	-1°02'
♅	19°♑32'	-0°25'
♆	19°♑31'	+0°40'
♇	25°♏21'	+14°22'
☊	18°♐43'	-0°00'
Mc	03°♈49'	-0°00'
As	20°♋31'	-0°00'

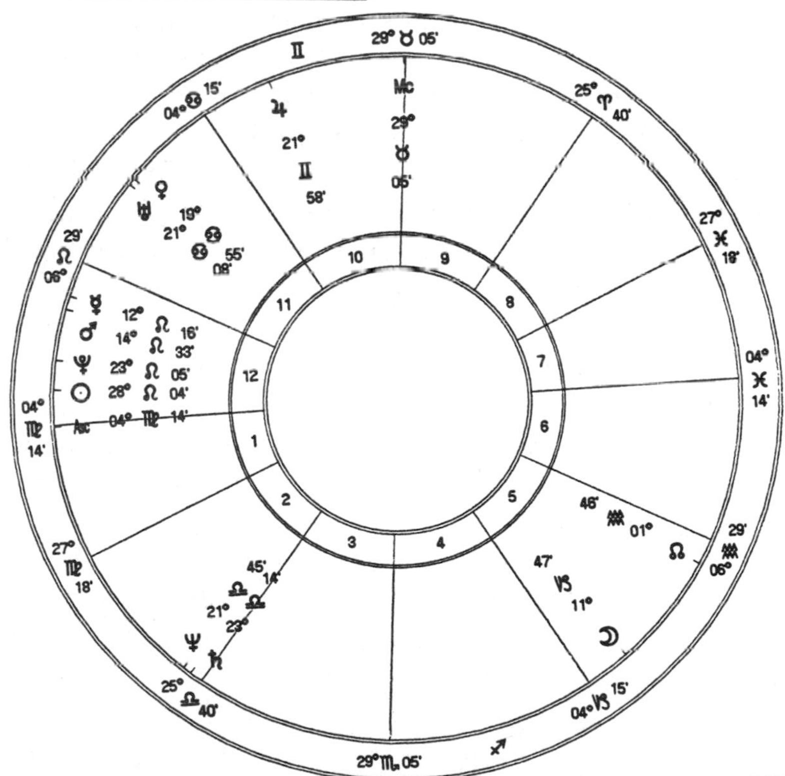

entire year traveling alone and as far as I knew, was still alone. In spite of this, I knew the predicted event would occur.

Two weeks later he called me regarding a book manuscript I had asked him to read for my company. One of the first things I said to him was "I'm sorry I didn't get a chance to call you earlier. I looked at your Chart a couple of weeks ago and it indicated that last week you should have fallen in love and proposed all on the same day."

He was taken back and paused for a moment. Then he became quite enthusiastic an said "I did! I couldn't believe it! But, I did!" He continued to explain how surprised he was about what he had done because it had all occurred on about the same day. He fell in love and proposed on the same day. Exactly as I had predicted.

There are three major factors that compose the scenario that brings about marriage: love, sexuality and commitment. The commitment itself is governed entirely by Transit Saturn's relationship to the Ruler of the 7th House. So, when predicting marriage, that is the first place you look. The other two factors are governed by the 5th House of Love and the 8th House of Sexuality. The two Transiting Planets that you look for to determine the conditions of these Houses are Saturn and Jupiter. Thus, the entire Marriage Scenario is composed of: Transit Saturn and Transit Jupiter acting on the 5th, 7th and 8th House Ruling Planets. However, it is Transit Saturn making a Soft Aspect to the 7th House Ruler that triggers the commitment. Thus, this Aspect is the starting point for predicting marriage.

Let's take a look at the Professor's Chart. For right now we'll study just the marriage part of the prediction. Once this comes into focus then we'll review love and sexuality. By the time you have completed this section, you will be able to easily study and predict all the basic elements leading to a committed relationship.

Last year when I pulled up his chart on my computer, this is what it looked like (see Chart #6 on page 65). Knowing that he was a bachelor, I was curious to see his Marriage Cycle. So, I found the Ruler of his 7th House and looked at its relationship to Transiting Saturn.

For review, put your finger on his Chart and follow this. His Natal Chart shows that the Cusp of his 7th House is in Pisces. Therefore the sign of Pisces Rules his 7th House. So, the Planet Neptune on his Natal Chart Rules his 7th House. Look at his Chart for the location of his Natal Neptune. Put a little "7" next to Neptune just to keep track of it.

Now that the Ruler of his 7th House has been located, the next step in marriage prediction is to determine its relationship to Transiting Saturn. On the top of Chart #6 are two tables. One table shows the position of his Transits on the day I looked at his Chart and the other shows the position of his Natal Planets. Using the Transit table, locate the position of Transiting Saturn and notate this on his Chart. Now, counting Signs (counter clockwise) from his Natal Neptune to Transit Saturn, there are four signs. (Note: In this Chart, Intercepted Signs are shown in the outside ring. Sagittarius is contained completely within his 4th House.) That's a Trine- a Soft Aspect. For a very available single guy, I'd call it a marriage Aspect!

Any Soft Aspect to the Ruler of the 7th House heralds the coming of a committed relationship. The exact way in which the relationship manifests is always dependent on the age, history, maturity, desire and readiness of the person whose Chart you are reading. In the case of my happy bachelor Professor friend, that meant marriage. On the other hand, if the bachelor or bachelorette had serious unhealed wounds from a recent relationship, rather than tying the knot, it may indicate that they simply have an exclusive relationship. They may live together or simply see each other on an exclusive basis. In doing so, they would be provided the opportunity to resolves past issues without the threat of formalized commitment through marriage.

When the same Aspect shows up in a preteen's Chart, it can create a committed best friend relationship. No matter what the exact nature of the committed relationship brought about through this Aspect, the tendency is always to formalize or mark the event in some external way. I have a striking example of this from a friend of mine. We were studying her Chart and found that when she was eleven years old, Transit Saturn made a Soft Aspect to the Ruler of her 7th House. She was too young for a boyfriend, so I asked if she had made a best friend at the time. She said yes. I asked if they had done anything to formalize the relationship. She said that at the time of the Soft Aspect they both pricked their fingers with a pin. By putting them together they became blood sisters. The Soft Aspect of Transit Saturn to the Ruler of the 7th House almost always indicates a commitment and some event marking the commitment. Note this when studying your own Chart. You might find that the first best friend you had, occurred under a Soft Aspect to the Ruler of your 7th House, and you somehow formalized the relationship at the time.

Most often, the first Soft Aspect to the Ruler of the 7th House that occurs between the ages of 20 and 27 brings about marriage. That is to say, once a person has matured beyond teens, they naturally enter this first marriage window. So, when predicting when a teenager is going to have their first (hopefully last) marriage, look to the first Soft Aspect made by Transit Saturn to their 7th House Ruling Planet. Take time now, to look at your 7th House Saturn Cycle and see if you followed this pattern.

Let's get back to the Professor. His chart had the correct

conditions for committing because Transit Saturn was making an Exact Trine to the Ruler of his 7th House. But, I wanted to also know the conditions for falling in love. If his Chart indicated correct falling in love conditions as well, that would give more weight to a marriage prediction.

Before you go further, fill out the House Rulership Form for the Professor below. This is always a first step when studying the Marriage Scenario.

House Rulership Form (for the Professor's Chart)

House	Ruling Sign	Ruling Planet	Location
5th (Love)	______	______	________
7th (Commitment)	______	______	________
8th (Sex)	______	______	________

Looking at his Chart, his 5th House is Ruled by Capricorn and Capricorn is Ruled by the Planet Saturn. So, Saturn on his Chart always governs 5th House matters of love. Put a little "5" next to the Saturn in his Chart.

When I looked at the Professor's Chart, what I noticed was that the Ruler of His 7th House of Commitment (his Natal Neptune) and the Ruler of his 5th House of Love (his Natal Saturn) were right up next to each other. They are only about one and a half degrees apart. Take a look at his Chart to see what I'm talking about. Because these two Planets are together (circle them) on his chart, all conditions concerning their House Rulership (the 5th House of Love and the 7th

House of Marriage) would occur pretty much at the same time. I had already noticed that Transiting Saturn was going to make an Exact Trine to his 7th House Ruler. That's how I saw the marriage part of the prediction. Because the Planet Ruling his 5th House of Love was right next door, I also knew that Saturn's restrictive power would act on that House in a very favorable way regarding matters of love. Saturn's restriction being delivered through a Soft Aspect to the Ruler of the 5th House could mean that his personal love would be restricted to one person.

But, that whole prediction is somewhat dry. Falling in love and getting married doesn't have much pizzazz until the scenario is acted upon by what many people consider the most lucky Transit: Jupiter. Jupiter's essence power is to expand. Through this, it brings about excess and abundance. In the Professor's Chart, I noticed that just about the same time Transit Saturn was to bring conditions favorable for marriage and love, Transiting Jupiter was going to Conjunct both the same Natal Planets on his Chart. (Take a look at the Transit Table to find the location of Transiting Jupiter. Mark its location on his Chart.) Transit Jupiter would bring the condition of his 5th House of Love and his 7th House of Marriage to a point of excessive bliss and Saturn would bring commitment.

As a sort of side note here, you might begin to see why people don't fall in love and get married all that often. The Astrological condition thus far in the Professor's Chart was a once in a lifetime event. The Planets would probably never line up like that again. The window created brought to him the woman of his dreams. I point this out because I want to make it clear that not any lady could just stumble into his life at that point. It had to be a mate that was in harmony with the forces at work. The desires and feelings brought about by the Transiting Planets don't open a person to remain in a vacuum. The Transiting Planets open you up and the natural result is to attract the circumstances in your life that are in resonance with the positions of the Transits.

The final piece of the Marriage Scenario concerns the ongoings of the 8th House of Sexuality. When I looked at his Chart and noticed all the other things, I also saw that Transiting Jupiter (the Planet that brings excess) was making a Soft Aspect to the Ruler of his 8th House (Neptune). This would bring him abundant and very pleasurable conditions in that area. Timing wise, all these events would reach their peak (the Transits would become Exact) at about the same time. The sum total of his Chart translates into the Ideal Marriage Scenario: Soft Aspects made by Transiting Jupiter and Saturn to the Ruling Planets of the 5th, 7th and 8th Houses.

7th HOUSE FALSE SEPARATION

When studying marriage you have to keep in mind the over all conditions of the subject. When Transit Saturn makes Soft Aspects to the Ruler of the 7th House, it creates conditions that are suitable to making a permanent commitment. But, the specific events that occur are entirely dependent on the individual. To give you an example, I had a young client call me to set an appointment for a reading. When he called he asked if he could bring his girlfriend so I could read both their Charts. I said yes. Before the appointment I studied both their Charts. I found that Transiting Saturn was beginning to make Soft Aspects to their 7th House Ruling Planet and that this was occurring in both Charts at the same time.

Just before his reading he called me to let me know that he would not be bringing his girlfriend. During the reading he told me that they had separated. Because of this and in spite of the fact that they had a child together, he felt that their was no hope for the relationship. I talked to him further and found that neither one of them had acted responsible toward the relationship and there was a history of drug abuse. They had never addressed many of their personal problems. Luckily neither he nor his girlfriend had any interest in outside relationships to complicate things further.

This is how I advised him. I told him that their Charts definitely indicated that they would make a marriage commitment to each other. That the separation was a result of an unhealthy way in dealing with a love relationship. Saturn always demands that a person act in a responsible fashion. When it Aspects the 7th House Ruling Planet, the conditions of that House will always surface and must be dealt with. It was the surfacing of buried issues that caused the separation. I told them that during separation they would have personal space to become emotionally clear and would come together occasionally to deal with past issues. I spoke to him sometime after the reading and the relationship proceeded as I predicted.

7th HOUSE ADULT BEST FRIENDS

Transiting Saturn making a Soft Aspect to the 7th House Ruler in an adult's Chart does not always indicate a committed relationship between opposite sexes. Even as an adult, this Aspect can be translated into a best friend relationship between the same sex. An example occurred in the Chart of a client of mine. Rather than forming a committed relationship with a man, a girlfriend of hers moved into her home. She is now her best friend. But, knowing her overall history and desires regarding committed relationships, this could have been predicted. Also, her Chart showed no coinciding 5th House or 8th House activity to justify marriage.

7th HOUSE LIMITED COMMITMENT

I have an old friend whose Chart indicated that she would be making a commitment. Again, Transiting Saturn was going to form a Soft Aspect to her 7th House Ruling Planet. Also, her Chart showed favorable Aspects to her 5th House and 8th House. These are very strong indicators of marriage, but I knew that she was still healing the wounds from her divorce. Because of this I did not believe that she was emotionally ready to make a full marriage commitment. As it happened, shortly after the 7th House Aspect became Exact she was in a committed relationship. She did not marry but enjoyed the company of her boyfriend on an exclusive basis. They see each other several times a week. The relationship is giving her the opportunity to work out the problems that had developed as a result of having been a co dependent in her prior marriage.

8th HOUSE MARRIAGE

I have a client who has been married several times. During her first reading we reviewed each of her marriages. When we got to the date of the third marriage I found that Saturn was not making any Aspect to the Ruler of her 7th House of Commitment. It was however making a Soft Aspect to the Ruler of her 8th House. When I saw this I said to her "It looks like you married for money. Is that what happened?" She said

"Yes, I married him for the financial security."

Along with sexuality, the 8th House Rules shared assets. When this shows up on the date of marriage, it means that the subject married for financial security. It's called an 8th House marriage. Because a commitment is not made to the individual, this type of marriage tends to not to last. The endings of an 8th House marriages can occur under a Hard Jupiter (not Saturn) Aspect to the 7th House Ruling Planet. On the other hand, if a *7th* House marriage ended, it would most likely occur under a Hard *Saturn* Aspect to the 7th House Ruler.

If you find an 8th House marriage in a Chart, it's important to not make value judgments. These commitments are important and have a definite purpose in both subject's lives.

SATURN THE FATHER PLANET

During a Soft Aspect by Transit Saturn to the Ruler of the 7th House, whatever is blocking commitment will be removed in order for a commitment to come about. As in one example above ("7th House False Separation"), the removal on the surface could appear to be an ending by initiating a separation. It is an ending only in the since that it ends issues blocking commitment. The events that lead up to commitment and the level of commitment are always dependent upon the profile of the subject being studied.

For thousands of years Saturn has been referred to by Astrologers as the Father Planet. It makes you work to grow. As the Planet of Restriction, it is a taskmaster. Marriage is an act of responsibility and Saturn will see it no other way.

THE CONJUNCTION

The Aspects determine the way in which the natural power

of a Planet is delivered. One of the unique features of the Conjunction, a Soft Aspect, is that it brings endings and beginnings. For predicting marriage this is quite important.

I have a friend who has been married twice. We went back to her first divorce and found that about the time Transiting Saturn was making a Conjunction to the Ruler of her 7th House, she left her husband. As you found, because a Conjunction is a Soft Aspect, it is the basis for predicting marriage. But many months before it became Exact, she left her husband. Then, just before the Aspect became Exact, she met and "fell in love" with the man she would spend the next ten years with. That is the nature of a Conjunction. It brings endings and beginnings. In the extreme situation the result is divorce and marriage. If the relationship is healthy and will continue, the Aspects would indicate that it will move to a higher or more mature level after ending some no longer needed part of the relationship.

Take time now to look back at your Chart (or any Charts you are studying). If this Aspect occurred, how did it effect your committed relationship(s)?

MANIFESTER PLANETS

There are two main Transiting Planets used in prediction. They are Saturn and Jupiter. Each one has a specific function for the Predictive Astrologer. As you found, Transiting Saturn can always be relied on as the beginning point for predicting marriage. Once a date for possible marriage has been found, then Transiting Jupiter is taken into consideration.

Both Transit Saturn and Transit Jupiter bring things about or cause events to occur. Although their more important and most powerful effects actually lay on a subtle, non-tangible level, they always cause tangible, identifiable and objectively verifiable events to come about. For that reason, together they are called the Manifester Planets.

THE OPPOSITION

The Opposition is a Hard Aspect. It creates challenges. The unique feature of this Aspect is that the conditions it brings forward are outside your direct control. That is, they usually are not a result of something that you did and you have little direct control over the manifestation itself. You do however have control over how you deal with the manifestation. Take a look at the Charts you are studying and see how this occured in your life.

MARRIAGE PREDICTION AND THE EVENT

In Predictive Astrology, the event of marriage is understood to be commitment. Marriage can imply the formalities of ceremony along with government regulated sanctions (license, blood tests, etc.). In prediction, these formalities are not considered a part of the personal commitment being made.

As discussed under the "Manifester Planets" above, the effects of Transit Saturn are far more reaching and much deeper than the formalities that celebrate the commitment itself. The Planets bring a person to a point on a psychological as well as emotional level and provide the environmental conditions necessary to make a personal one-on-one commitment. The apex of that process occurs when the Transit becomes Exact for the last time. Whether or not the formalities occur on the same date is dependent on the individual and the particular circumstances of the individual subject being studied. So, when predicting marriage you should always find that the personal commitment was made approximately on the date the Aspect became Exact for the last time and was somehow outwardly symbolized at that time. The formal ceremonies and government sanctions, however, may or may not occur on the same date.

MULTIPLE HITS

Sometimes a Transiting Planet goes Retrograde. That is, from our perspective here on Earth it appears to move backward in the sky. As a result, the Transit can make the same Aspect three times: once on its first pass, once after it has gone Retrograde and once after it again goes Direct. Although the predicted event could come about on any one of the passes, it is the last hit that usually is timed with the predicted event. The first two hits serve to bring to the surface issues that ultimately lead to the final event that occurs on the final hit. So in predicting the date of the event, use the date of the final hit.

CHART RECTIFICATION

The first step in prediction is to make sure that you have the correct Birth Data. A birth time difference of ten minutes will not effect the position of the Planets in a significant way. The slowest moving Planet is the Moon and would move only six minutes in ten minutes of time. But, a ten minute change in birth time changes the position of the Houses by about four degrees. Moving the House Lines that much can often put the Cusp of the House in a different Sign. That would change the

Planet that Rules the House. So, the first order of business when predicting is to rectify the Chart. The most frequently used method and easiest way to do so is exactly what you did in the "Seventh House Saturn Study." Simply flip through the Emphemeris finding the years when Saturn was making Aspects to the 7th House Ruling Planet. While doing this, find out if any major change occurred in the committed relationship area and if the change followed the nature of the Aspects. (Soft Aspects/beginnings and Hard Aspects/challenges.) If the overall pattern is followed, then you can pretty much consider the Chart rectified.

If you do not know the birth time, you can work backward. Simply find out the dates of major changes (marriage, separation, etc.) and then look at the Natal Chart to find out what Planet Transiting Saturn is making Aspect to. If the general pattern points to one Planet, then you can pretty much figure that Planet is the 7th House Ruling Planet.

Chart rectification can get quite detailed and complex. But, the above serves as an excellent guideline.

ORBS

When a Transiting Planet comes to within a specified number of degrees of becoming Exact, it is said to be in Orb. The number of degrees varies from Astrologer to Astrologer and according to the Planets involved. The topic of Orbs itself is complex, meaningful and debatable. In general however, a Transiting Planet coming within 10 degrees of Exact can be considered in Orb. For prediction, events that lead up to the predicted event should begin to occur when the Transit comes into a 10 degree Orb.

The Orb exists on both sides of the Natal Planet. So, after

the Aspect becomes Exact and moves away from the Natal Planet, it is still considered to be in Orb until it passes 10 degrees beyond.

When the Aspect is headed toward the Natal Planet, the Orb is decreasing is size. In this position it is considered a Waning Orb. Once the Aspect passes the Natal Planet, the Orb is increasing. In this position, it is called a Waxing Orb.

7th HOUSE COMMITMENT TO SELF

Transiting Saturn making a Soft Aspect to the 7th House Ruler brings about conditions suitable for commitment. The nature of the commitment is always dependent upon the need and readiness of the subject. I have a professional Astrologer friend who under this Aspect came to the realization that she had overlooked herself in the marriage process. That is, somehow in her recent prior marriage by giving herself over to her husband, she had not been true to her self. What she needed was a stronger commitment to herself and under this Aspect she moved off on her own to gain personal strength through self-commitment.

SLOW AND FAST MOVING PLANETS

The two Transits you have studies thus far are Saturn and Jupiter. There are three more that you will begin to study in the next Chapter. Every Planet requires a specific amount of time to travel around the Zodiac. This time ranges from 30 days for the Moon to 248 years for Transiting Pluto. As a result, the Transiting Planets are grouped into two categories: Fast Moving and Slow Moving.

The Table below shows the amount of time required by each Planet for one complete revolution around the Zodiac and the division between Fast and Slow Moving Planets.

Table #6 - Planets Revolution Time

Fast Moving Planets		***Slow Moving Planets***	
Planet	*Aprox time for one revolution*	*Planet*	*Aprox time for one revolution*
Moon	30 days	Jupiter	12 years
Sun	1 year	Saturn	29 years
Mercury	88 days	Uranus	84 years
Venus	225 days	Neptune	165 years
Mars	2 years	Pluto	248 years

TRIGGERS

The Exact time that a predicted event will occur quite often is the time when the Aspect made by Transiting Saturn (or whatever Transit is being used for prediction) becomes Exact for the last time. However, sometimes when the Waxing or Waning Orb of the Transit used for prediction comes to within 3 or 4 degrees of Exact, a Slow Moving Planet can enter the Orb and Trigger the event.

In entering the Orb, it does not have to actually move into a Conjunction position to the Natal Planet. It merely has to create it's own Orb to the Natal Planet by positioning itself somewhere in the Zodiac.

The exact timing of the event using one Trigger Planet is

when the Trigger Planet's Aspect becomes Exact. If two or more Fast Moving Planets are involved with Triggering an event, it is when their combined forces are closest to becoming Exact. The calculation involved for this situation is beyond the scope of this book. It is however important for you to know at this point that Fast Moving Planets can Trigger the predicted event. Thus, the exact date of the event may not be the exact date Transiting Saturn or Jupiter becomes Exact.

To study the triggering effect of Slow Moving Planets, you need a complete Ephemeris that lists the locations of all Planets on a daily basis. You can purchase one for about $25 in the Astrological section of any bookstore.

HOUSE CUSPS

One of the most powerful tools in Predictive Astrology revolves around House Cusps. When a Slow Moving Planet Conjuncts a House Cusp, all issues concerning the House are immediately brought forward in an obvious, profound and striking manner. The way in which they are brought forward is defined by the Essence Power of the Transit. The condition of the issues which come forward are according to where the subject left them on last consideration. The issues tone down after the Transit enters a few degrees of the House but remain present in the subject's life to be processed by him/her until the Transit exits the House. A few degrees prior to exit, there can be a minor "flair up" mirroring any unfinished business initiated by the House Conjunction.

If a Slow Moving Planet Conjuncts a House Cusp and at about the same time a Slow Moving Planet makes an Aspect to the Ruling Planet of the same House, major life changes and/or challenges occur according to the House, Aspect and Transits involved. For example, in 1993 Transiting Uranus Conjuncted Barbra Streisand's 11th House Cusp and about the same time Transiting Pluto Opposed her 11th House Ruler. The results thus far have been her ending a 28-year period in which she did not sing publicly. The 11th House governs large groups of people.

Another example revolves around the Chart of the boyfriend of a client. Transit Pluto Conjuncted his 12th House Cusp and at the same time, Transiting Saturn made an Opposition to his 12th House Ruling Planet. None of these Aspects would be considered light or favorable. Pluto is often considered the God of Hell, the 12th House governs institutions such as prisons and Saturn restricts. Saturn being in Opposition would indicate that the event(s) would be a result of an innocent act or something outside of the subject's control. As it happened, while intoxicated, he got into a small boat to help a friend whose yacht was stuck under a drawbridge that had failed to open. The Coast Guard was alerted and came to assist. When they found him intoxicated he was cited for drunk boating. This was his second offense. About the time the Aspects became Exact he entered county jail for a five months stay.

THE DELAYED JUPITER EFFECT

If Transiting Jupiter makes a Soft Aspect to the 7th House Ruling Planet after Transiting Saturn, often the effect is as follows: The personal commitment is made on the date Transit Saturn becomes Exact. Commitment can almost always be predicted by this Aspect. However, the celebration of the commitment (wedding) could occur about the time Transiting Jupiter becomes Exact.

This is useful when comparing two Charts. It could occur that there is a large amount of time between two Charts having Saturn make Soft Aspects to their 7th House Rulers. Even with positive 5th and 8th House activity, because of the time difference concerning the 7th House Saturn Aspect, the prediction would be: The subjects being studied would make commitments but not with each other. However, if the Delayed Jupiter Effect is in operation, and timed with both Charts, then marriage could occur between the two subjects.

NOTATION

It helps to have a system of notation that captures all the necessary Chart information in brevity. That way you can see the overview of pertinent information at a glance.

Notation is a very personal process. You are probably better off developing your own system based on your own perspective. However, I will show you one that seems to work most of the time. The unfortunate side effect of notation is that it could tend to perpetuate the notion that somehow the event being studied is an isolated part of the subject's life. Sort of like thinking that one part of your body exists separately from the whole.

Study the following notation and use it if it feels comfortable to you.

12/24/94 T♄△N☿ (7,=3)4♋ +1°

On 12/24/94 Transiting Saturn will Trine Natal Mercury, which Rules the 7th House and Co-Rules the 3rd House. The Natal Planet is located in the 4th house in the Sign of Cancer. On 12/24/94 the Aspect will have a Waxing Orb of 1 degree.

THE MARS CYCLE

Mars takes about two years to travel around the Zodiac. Because it is a Fast Moving Planet, it can act to Trigger (see page 80) events predicted through the use of the Manifester Planets (Saturn and Jupiter). In addition to its Triggering effect, it creates a very important two year cycle of its own.

The essence power of Transiting Mars acts on the basic drive force of the individual. As a result, the Mars Cycle represents your Drive Cycle. I've discussed this with clients before and one of the first questions asked is "What do you mean by drive?" They usually are satisfied when I say it's the strong feeling you have to get something done. On the other hand, depending on your overall nature, Mars can also bring out violence, your sexual drive, creative drive or any other drive you have. If they still don't get it, I say "Imagine a world where people have no desire to do anything; they just sit around all day spaced out and you have imagined a planetary system with no Mars." Mars is your Drive force. It manifests like clockwork according to the Aspects it makes and when it makes them.

When you feel you're ready, perhaps after completing the next Chapter, I highly recommend that you take time to study your Mars Cycle. Mars is included in the abbreviated Ephemeris in the back of the book and you can use one of the extra Study Forms to keep track of the Aspects. It's difficult to go back in time to study the effects of Mars, so I suggest that you simply make a list of the dates Transiting Mars Aspects become Exact and study them as they occur. If you are not on a tight budget, you can simply order your Mars Cycle by using the form in the back of the book.

Chapter Four

ALL SLOW TRANSITS

Thus far you have studied the effects and powers of only the Manifester Planets, Jupiter and Saturn. When you are predicting events, they are the first Transits to examine. However, the remaining three Slow Moving Planets (Uranus, Neptune and Pluto) have a profound and powerful impact on our lives as well. They should always be considered along with the Manifester planets.

For prediction, first look to the Manifester Planets to tell you what the event will be and then to the remaining Slow

Moving Planets to tell you under what conditions the event will manifest. For example, I have a friend whose Chart showed that both Transiting Jupiter and Saturn were going to be Trining the Ruler of her 2nd House of Money. Thus, she was entering a high income cycle. Because both Jupiter and Saturn were making Soft Aspects at about the same time, this would probably be thc highest income period she had experienced. I wanted to know the conditions under which this would come about. So, I studied the positions of Uranus, Neptune and Pluto. I found that Uranus was going to make an exact Conjunction to the ruler of her 10th House of Career a few months before her 2nd House activity. Transiting Uranus's essence power is catalytic; it accelerates. This catalytic acceleration most often manifests as surprising and unexpected changes in House affairs. Considering the two Aspects together, it indicated that she was going to have an extreme increase in her personal income as a result of a sudden and unexpected career change.

I was concerned that she may feel hesitant about making any career changes so I called her. When she got on the phone, I told her that she would be making an unexpected career change and assured her that it would be beneficial for her financially. Later she told me that "out of the clear blue" a friend had arranged a dinner for her in which she was introduced to the owner of a company for the purpose of working for him. After the social interview, she accepted the new position. She was quite nervous about the change in particular because it came so fast and was unexpected but was comforted from my call. She went from making $30,000 a year as an employee for a company to earning $85,000 a year doing the same work as an independent contractor. It was a sudden and unexpected positive change of career leading to higher income, exactly as I had predicted.

It is not within the scope of this book to offer an in depth study of the remaining Planets or Houses. However, this Chapter will give you the opportunity to begin their study. Refer to the Appendices in the back of the book for further information about specific House matters and Planet powers.

Before you begin, it should be noted that the path of the Planets are elliptical. For the three Planets discussed in this chapter, this makes a significant difference. For example, Uranus has been moving more quickly though the Zodiac. Thus, the Opposition it forms at an estimated age of 42 comes much earlier now. This Opposition is associated with midlife crisis which now occurs at about age 38.

URANUS

Uranus essence power is catalytic. It derives its power through its connection with infinite mind. The relationship between man and his understanding of time ceases to operate under its influence. It's power is higher mind and in relationship to time, it appears as instant knowingness; simply knowing without need of logic or processs. Intuition is associated with this Planet along with genius. It is the higher octave of the Fast Moving Planet Mercury, which governs logic. Thus, they work together or are in harmony with each other. As a Transit, its effect is catalytic. So much so that its effects are dramatic and surprising.

Each Planet produces definitive cycle based on Aspects made to itself over time. The cycles they create occur regardless of what Houses the particular Planet Rules in your Natal Chart. The cycles have a character of their own. However, it is not within the context of this book to spend a lengthy amount of time discussing the cycles of each Planet. However, for the beginning predictive Astrologer, it is quite important that you understand that they do exist, and of the ten cycles created by each Planet unto itself, you should have an understanding of the cycles of Uranus.

Uranus revolves around the Zodiac about once every 84 years. Depending upon how old you live to be, it can make one complete revolution thus touching every aspect of your life in every way it can. The cycles it creates are associated with maturation. The first Aspect occurs when it forms a Sextile to itself at about age fourteen. This aspect coincides with becoming a teenager. Knowing that the essence power of Uranus acts as a catalyst and its power is most closely associated with knowingness without logic, its first expression through teenhood as the stereotypic "know-it-all" attitude makes sence. For someone who was most recently a ten year old child, it is a major challenge and acts as a right of passage to becoming a young adult.

The next Aspect it makes unto itself is at about age 21. During that cycle it Squares itself, thus creating internal challenges tied to its essence power. For the 21-year old, this usually shows up and revolves around the process of self-assertion in a socialized environment for the purpose of creating an income. Thus, the young man or woman first integrates into society as an adult at this point. There is conflict between what they know inwardly and what is expected of them by the structure they enter. It is at this point and on this issue that the individual is tested. The outcome of this test defines their relationship with the structure in which they live. A clear direction or pattern of the individual as an adult is formed under this challenge. In this sence, it is the end of childhood and the beginning of adulthood.

At about age 28, Uranus makes a Trine unto itself which can manifest as a sence of adjustment to adulthood. The whole inward knowingness process, all things being equal, should be harmony with itself and the surrounding social structure in which it functions.

Then about fourteen years pass before it makes the next Aspect. At about age 38 or 39, it forms an Opposition. During this period you're given the opportunity to examine and resolve any past matters dealing with your maturation process. Because it is an Opposition, when I said "you are given," I meant that quite literally. The nature of an Opposition is that the events which occur are not a result of action that you initiated. Things just happen and there is nothing you can do to prevent them from occurring. However, the way in which you choose to deal with the events and feelings that unfold during this period are under you control. The whole process in its extreme manifestation has traditionally been called mid-life crisis.

A classic example of this is the male who buys a fast, red Italian sports car, starts dressing groovy, falls in love and has a wild affair with a teenager. All of this is symptomatic of unsatisfied needs from teenhood. If questioned about the period of his life associated with the age of his lover, he would probably reveal that he felt rejected by the girls in his school and out of place because he did not fit into the groovy "in" crowd.

During the Uranus Opposition unresolved or unsatisfied issues come forward to be reexamined. The situations associated with the issues play themselves out again. It's sort of like a rerun of a film, but you have the opportunity to edit the parts that you were unhappy about. Knowing that the whole process is an important and crucial healing cycle helps to deal with extreme situations. Not allowing the healing process can create an emotionally disabled adult who missed the last dosage of vaccine that could have prepared him for entry into middle age.

I know of one professional Astrologer who during the Aspect found himself in his backyard building a tree house. In so doing he was healing a deficit from his childhood. Thus, a healing of old issues occurred. I have another friend who under this Aspect spent three years sampling every lady of the night in our city. He was able to offer sophisticated, informative and interesting critiques of the various establishments and ladies in our town along with the details of their intimate services. His focus was women in their early twenties, which reflected the difficulties he had socially after graduating from college.

The outward manifestations do not always show up as dramatically. But, they always reflect inward needs that have gone unsatisfied or unhealed during the growing process. It is the emotion of dissatisfaction that is the revealing clue. Once the dissatisfaction is associated with an outward event and the event can be seen as a reflection of some past unresolved issue, the healing process is well underway.

I have another client who during this period found himself probing his entire life and consciously healing the unresolved issues he found. He spent three years focused on this process. The entire scenario reflected the fact that he had come from a "trauma drama" family that prevented him from healing as he moved forward though his youth.

As an effort to aid in the healing process during this Aspect, associate the events that unfold with specific past periods of life. Thus, if you find yourself building a tree house, ask the question "At what age were tree houses an issue in my life?" This will cue you as to the wound you are healing, which was created by some sort of lack. Whatever happens, happens under this Aspect and ultimately the events simply play themselves out. This is definitely not a time to become judgmental. It is a last opportunity for healing certain issues. In that sence, it is a right of passage into midlife.

The next Aspect is the Trine which occurs at about age 54. This favorable Aspect represents an apex in the growth process. During this Aspect one should feel at home with themselves and at ease with their own natures.

The next Aspect comes at about age 63. The main conflict that occurs during this Square revolves around the individual and their relationship with society. The sence that you are no longer needed or wanted in the working world comes forth.

Then at about age 70 the Sextile appears again. But, this time rather than as a "know-it-all" teenager, the knowingness power of Uranus puts one closer in touch with higher spiritual vibrations. This is associated with "The golden years."

The final aspect of the cycle is the return of the Conjunction at age 84. From this final Aspect, great wisdom comes forth through the association of life's experiences with simply knowing. This is the wisdom of age.

Not everyone lives to the final Uranus Conjunction. Fewer still live beyond this to the next Sextile which arrives at about age 98. This aspect reaches deeper into knowingness and wisdom yet somehow continues to speak the language of the material world. If you have ever talked to anyone that age you'll understand what I mean. Ask them a question about life, your life, and their words will resonate with eternal wisdom.

STUDY EXERCISE - Uranus

In this Study Exercise you are going to examine three effects of Uranus in you life: the Aspects made to itself, the

Aspects made to your various House Ruling Planets and the Aspects made to your House Cusps.

Step #1

Using the Ephemeris in the back of the book, note the position of Transiting Uranus about five years ago. Then, note the position of Uranus about three years from now. Mark these locations on the Zodiac wheel provided. (Note: If you ordered "The Works," skip to Step #3 below.)

Step #2

Compare the Planets in your Natal Chart to the path of Uranus. Find what Aspects were made during this period to your

STUDY FORM - Uranus

Month/Year	Aspect/RH	Comment
__________	_______	
__________	_______	
__________	_______	
__________	_______	
__________	_______	
__________	_______	
__________	_______	
__________	_______	
__________	_______	
__________	_______	
__________	_______	
__________	_______	
__________	_______	
__________	_______	
__________	_______	
__________	_______	

Natal Planets. Also, note if it Conjuncted any of your House Cusps. In addition to this, you may want to note any Aspects made by Transiting Uranus to your Natal Uranus. Mark the

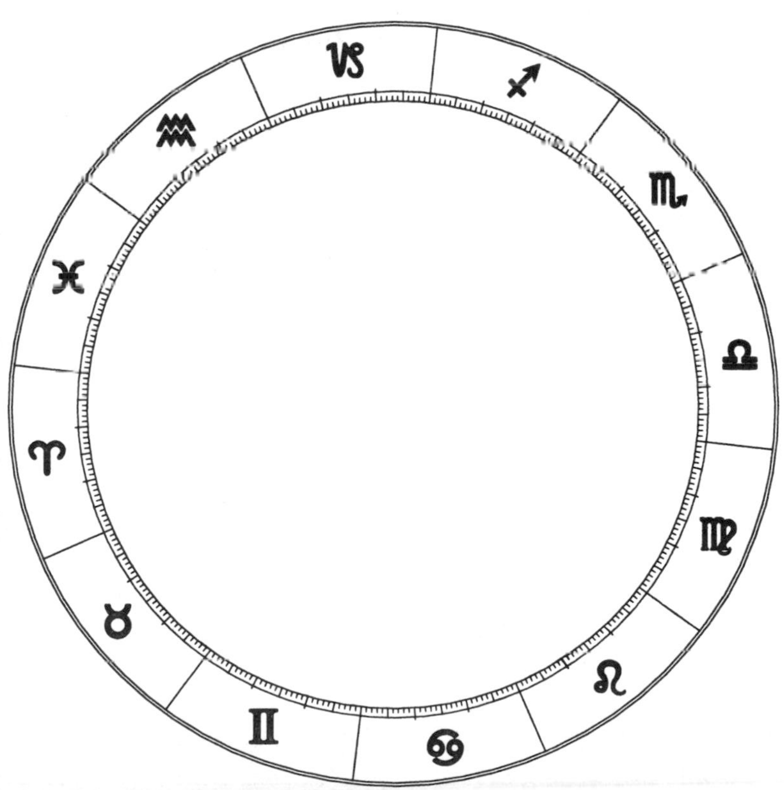

position of Transit Uranus on the Zodiac Wheel for all Aspects you select to study.

Step #3

Using the Ephemeris in the back of the book, look up the month and year when Transiting Uranus made/makes the Aspects found in the above step. Write these and Planets Ruling Houses (RH) into the appropriate place in the Study Form. If you ordered "The Works," simply select the Aspects you wish to study and transcribe this information into your Study Form.

Step #4

In the Comment section of your Study Form, notate any

STUDY FORM - Uranus

Month/Year	Aspect/RH	Comment
____________	________	
____________	________	
____________	________	
____________	________	
____________	________	
____________	________	
____________	________	
____________	________	
____________	________	
____________	________	
____________	________	
____________	________	
____________	________	
____________	________	
____________	________	
____________	________	

changes in your life that correspond with the forces of Uranus in relationship to the Aspects made. Use Appendix #2 to determine House matters affected.

Step #5
Review the Comments.

Prediction - Uranus

Because Uranus takes about 84 years to travel around the Zodiac, it represents one complete life cycle for man. For the Predictive Astrologer, it will always indicate major turnarounds regarding the House Ruling Planet to which it is making Aspect. When predicting events, it is also important to pay attention to its relationship to House Cusps. Although all Major Aspects have an effect on House Cusps, the most striking and obvious changes occur when a Slow Moving Planet makes an Exact Conjunction to a House Cusp.

PLUTO

Pluto has the deepest effect of all the Planets. Its energy operates on a subconscious level connecting with the deepest hidden parts of our personal makeup. It presents this information to us on an emotional, mental and spiritual level according to the Aspects involved. Under Soft Aspects, this comes forward as personal revolution of our deepest selves in a more inspirational and desirable manner. Under Hard Aspects, parts of our selves and issues that we may not know exist and may not want to examine are surfaced under its influence. The Soft Aspects are associated with great healing and personal revelation. The Hard Aspects are associated with death. Over the period of one lifetime, Pluto's force is associated with presenting us with some of our greatest challenges and in the process deepening and strengthening our personal character.

Death does not exits unto itself. Death is always associated with birth. In order to die, one is reborn. This process occurs on all levels. So, no matter what Aspect Pluto is making, it involves a death and a birth. The summation of this power is transformation. The details of the transformation are tied into the Aspects being made.

Unfortunately, its influence can be so deep and so heavy that it is easy to overlook the birth involved. Thus, quite often the death part of the process becomes the center of focus. This occurs in particular under a Hard Aspect. However, under the Soft Aspect, a higher understanding focused on the birth side of the transformation is more readily available.

I have a client whose husband recently had open heart surgery. I looked at her Chart and found that Pluto was making a Trine to the ruler of her 7th House of Marriage thus indicating transformation (death and rebirth) that would be focused around her relationship with her husband. She has been married to the same man for many years and has always been devoted to him as a wife.

The relationship she has had with him can been seen as one where she has spiritual understanding and he does not. He has always been closed to ideas of spiritual guides, reincarnation, angels, etc.

During his triple bypass surgery he died clinically for about one minute. Being intuitive, she felt this as a loss while she was at the hospital and thought her husband had passed away during surgery. When the doctors came out, she expected them to announce his death to her. However, they advised her that the surgery was a complete success but mentioned that during the operation his vital signs had ceased for about one minute.

When her husband was awake and able to talk, he told her that during the operation he found himself standing next to his body trying to decide if he should live or die. His decision was to live, so he reentered his body. This was his first spiritual experience. Thus, the death part of the transformation bought about by this Aspect was the death of an old part of her husband-one that was unable to accept spiritual matters. The birth was spiritual realization. The sum total created a situation that brought them closer together and their closeness revolved around the birth part of the transformation.

That story is a good example of the lighter side of Pluto. Deep personal spiritual transformation brought about without major internal conflict allowing one to easily focus on the birth part of the transformation. A Soft Pluto Aspect. Tears may come forward but they are the kind of tears more closely associated with birth, weddings and realization of spiritual matters. Under a Soft Pluto Aspect, you experience your unconsciousness personal beliefs concerning God.

The heavier side of Pluto's energy is stirred up under Hard Aspects and can connect you with more challenging concerns-one's personal unconscious beliefs about the Devil. I have a friend who has had a girlfriend for several years. During a Square being made to the ruler of his 5th House of Love he came to me for a reading. He said he had been having problems with his relationship and on several occasions thought that she was the Devil. I explained to him that he was feeling the nature of the Pluto Aspect and it would pass. I affirmed for him that she was not the Devil- that there was no Devil. There is however a personal summation of what the Devil may be, and she was portraying that part in his life while Pluto was bringing this to the conscious level of his mind.

It is not always the case that the effects of Pluto are so dramatic. Most recently under an Opposition to the Ruler of her

10th House of Career, Barbra Streisand had to cancel her Anaheim concert due to laryngitis. Her voice died. The death was outside of her personal control, which is the nature of an Opposition. Most certainly her tour, which earned her over 40 million dollars, did not die. Nor did she. However, it may be that she was undergoing major personal transformation wherein she viewed herself and her entire career as some sort of Devil, and probably didn't know why she was thinking about this.

You cannot predict death simply because Pluto is making a Hard Aspect to some Natal Planet. Pluto's essence power is Transformation and it operates on the deepest levels involving death and rebirth. In order for something to be born, something else must cease to exist. But, what is dying and what is being born is dependent on the overall characteristics of the subject being studied and the exact Aspects being made. If a mortal death does occur, it is probably under the influence of Pluto. Pluto, among other things has been nicknamed "Planet of Death" and "God of Hell" simply because these sorts of events occur under its Aspect. But, because it is making Aspect does not mean that they will occur.

As a final example of the more challenging side of Pluto, most emotional breakdowns occur under its influence during Hard Aspects; in particular Squares and most often when Pluto is Squaring the Natal Moon, which governs all feelings, and/or Natal Mercury, which governs the ability to think, speak and reason. This occurs regardless of which Houses these two Natal Planets govern. I have a client who shortly after graduating from college twenty years ago had Pluto make three Exact Squares to his Natal Mercury. By the time it was over, he had seen demons, thought he was possessed, was "hearing voices," had frequented a local exorcist, was having visions, his mother died, he lost his girlfriend, had a major car accident, lost all his friends and had gone from 150 pounds to 118 pounds. This sort of extreme situation can not be predicted simply by the Aspect being made. It depends on the overall conditions of the subject being studied. In his situation, without going into depth, he had worked his way through college and quite simply was exhausted from the effort. As a result, he was not in any condition to deal properly with these forces when they arrived in his life.

STUDY EXERCISE - Pluto

Because Pluto takes about 248 years to travel around the Zodiac, it never makes a complete revolution in one's life. Thus, its influence is felt only for the Aspects made. To have

STUDY FORM - Pluto

Month/Year	Aspect/RH	Comment
________	________	
________	________	
________	________	
________	________	
________	________	
________	________	
________	________	
________	________	
________	________	
________	________	
________	________	
________	________	
________	________	
________	________	
________	________	

a complete understanding of Pluto, you must study several Charts.

<u>Step #1</u>

Using the Ephemeris in the back of the book, note the position of Transiting Pluto about five years ago. Then, note the position of Pluto about three years from now. Mark these locations on the Zodiac wheel provided. (Note: If you ordered "The Works," skip to Step #3 below.)

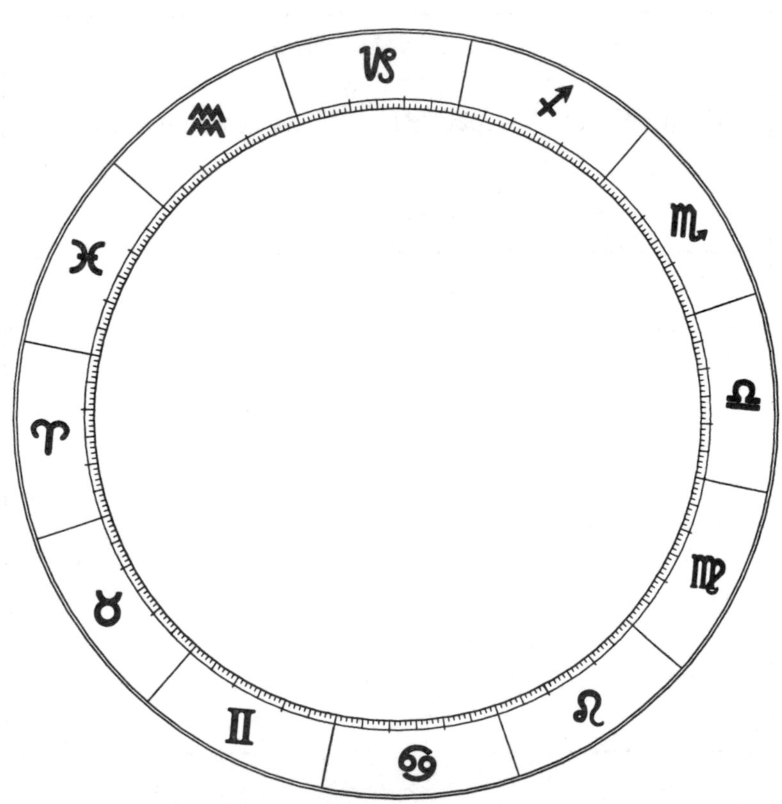

Step #2

Compare the Planets in your Natal Chart to the path of Pluto. Find what Aspects were made during this period. Note also if Pluto Conjuncted any of your House Cusps. Notate the position of Pluto on the Zodiac Wheel for any additional Aspects you study. You may want to study your Chart and see if Transiting Pluto has ever made a Square to your Natal Mercury or Natal Moon.

Step #3

Using the Ephemeris in the back of the book, look up the month and year when Transiting Pluto was making the Aspects found in the above step. Write these into the appropri-

STUDY FORM - Pluto

Month/Year	Aspect/RH	Comment
________	________	
________	________	
________	________	
________	________	
________	________	
________	________	
________	________	
________	________	
________	________	
________	________	
________	________	
________	________	
________	________	
________	________	
________	________	
________	________	

ate place along with House Rulers (RH) in the Study Form. If you ordered "The Works," simply select the Aspects you wish to study and transcribe this information into your Study Form.

Step #4

In the Comment section of your Study Form, notate any changes in your life that correspond with the forces of Pluto.

Step #5

Review the Comments to study how Pluto influenced your life. Use Appendix Two to study House matters effected.

Prediction - Pluto

Pluto is the slowest of all the Planets. Thus, the influence of the Aspects it creates are very long and last for many years. Its essence power is one of deep personal Transformation. Keeping this in mind while using Appendix Two to determine House matters that may be effected, study the current and future Aspects of this Planet. If you have any Hard Aspects coming up, then prepare your life accordingly. Make sure your House affairs are in order before the cycle begins, thus minimizing any discomfort you may experience. During the cycle and specifically when the Aspect becomes Exact, use the better parts of yourself and the support of your friends to keep things on an even keel with regard to the House matters being effected. As a Predictive Astrologer, you can also rely on the events surrounding any Soft Aspects made by other Slow Planets as your support Houses during Pluto's Aspects.

NEPTUNE

Unlike all the other Planets discussed so far, Neptune offers little help for the prediction of tangible events. It works on a higher level.

The essence power of Neptune acts as a solvent. That is, it serves to dissolve issues, not create them. In a simple way, it's like an eraser. During the process one can feel quite detached from normal reality. If this detachment is recognized as spiritual development, the whole process becomes more meaningful.

For a more complete review of Neptune's power, read the Planet section in the back of the book (Appendix One) before you do this study exercise.

STUDY EXERCISE - Neptune

The nature of the energy of Neptune makes it difficult to study. Going back in time to determine the date in which some-

STUDY FORM - Neptune

Month/Year	Aspect/RH	Comment
____________	________	
____________	________	
____________	________	
____________	________	
____________	________	
____________	________	
____________	________	
____________	________	
____________	________	
____________	________	
____________	________	
____________	________	
____________	________	
____________	________	
____________	________	
____________	________	

STUDY FORM - Neptune

Month/Year	Aspect/RH	Comment

thing dissolved is sort of like trying to recall when you forgot something. It takes about 164 years for it to revolve around the Zodiac. As a result, the cycles it creates are long which makes it even more challenging for the beginning student to pinpoint its effects in their lives.

Step #1

Using the Ephemeris in the back of the book, find the location of Neptune about five years ago and about three years from now. Mark these locations on the Zodiac Wheel provided. (Note: If you purchased "The Works" skip to step #3 .)

Step #2

Determine all Aspects that were made to your Natal Planets during Transiting Neptune's path marked on the Zodiac Wheel. Include any House Cusps that were Conjuncted.

Step #3

Using the Ephemeris in the back of the book, determine the month and year the above Aspects were Exact. Notate this along with the Ruling Houses (RH) in the appropriate sections of your Study Form. (Note: If you ordered "The Works" simply transcribe the information onto your Study Form. Add the Ruling House for each Natal Planet.)

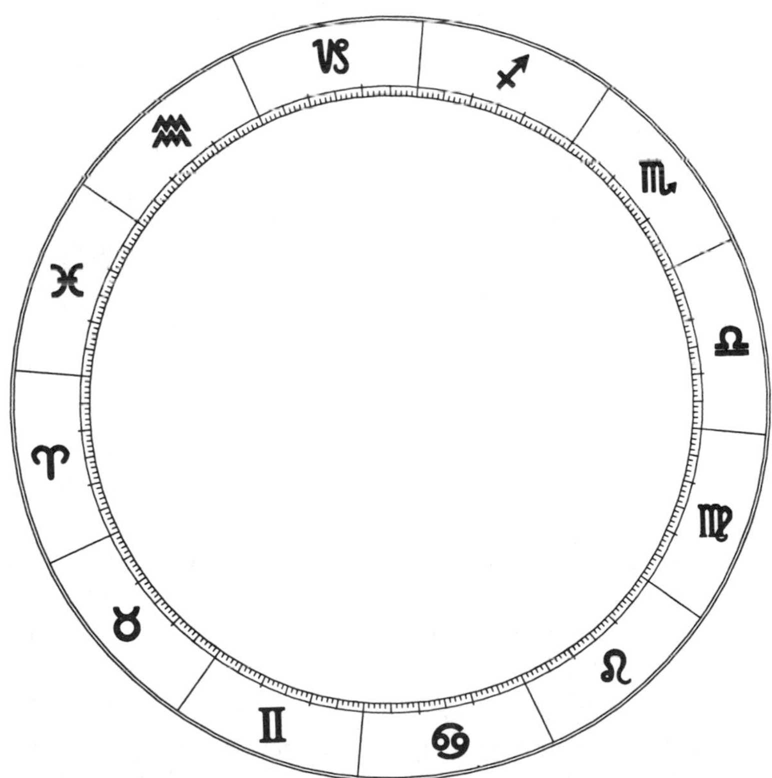

Step #4

Notate in the Comment Section of the Study Form any issues that you would associate with Neptune's energy.

Prediction - Neptune

Using Appendix Two, examine your Study Form to determine Neptune's effect in your life. Based on your discoveries, study the forthcoming Aspects.

PUTTING IT ALL TOGETHER

At this point you have had a chance to study all the Slow Moving Planets: Saturn, Jupiter, Uranus, Neptune and Pluto. Each has its effects on the cycles of our lives. When predicting, the first place to look is the Manifester Planets; Jupiter and Saturn. Then, once you have a fix on the House matters that these two Planets are acting on, the next step is to study the remaining Slow Moving Planets.

The Manifester Planets are used to determine the events, and the remaining Slow Moving Planets are used to determine the way in which or the tone under which the events will manifest. For example, the Manifester Planet Saturn may be making a Trine to the 7th House Ruling Planet. This could indicate the beginning of a committed relationship. Meanwhile, Transiting Jupiter may be Conjuncting the Ruler of the 8th House of Sex and at the same time Sextiling the 5th House Ruling Planet. That set of Transits pretty much defines the Ideal Marriage Scenario. To determine the over all conditions under which a marriage/commitment may come about, study the remaining Slow Moving Planets. In doing so, you may find that prior to the Saturn marriage Aspect, Transiting Uranus will be Conjuncting the Ruler of the 9th House. That Aspect would indicate surprising and immediate

9th House changes regarding long distance travel, spiritual development, higher education, ect. Thus, this information would somehow have to be a part of the prediction. Meanwhile, you note that Transiting Pluto is going to Trine the 5th House Ruling Planet one year after the predicted date of marriage. This would indicate that the subject would be entering one of his/her deepest cycles regarding who they love and who loves them. This would become a part of the overall marriage prediction as well and probably indicate that the person who they are going to marry is going to surface the subject's deepest feelings regarding love. Rather than offering a lengthy example, study your own Chart. Also, study the Chart of someone you know.

STUDY FORM - Putting It All Together

Month/Year	Aspect/RH	Comment
________	________	
________	________	
________	________	
________	________	
________	________	
________	________	
________	________	
________	________	
________	________	
________	________	
________	________	
________	________	
________	________	
________	________	
________	________	
________	________	

After working through the following Study Exercise you may want to read the case study in Chapter 5. It focuses on Barbra Streisand's Chart and includes all major commitments she has made. She definitely has been true to her Chart and will be married/committed again in March or December of 1995. The case study will reveal further insights into predictive Astrology.

STUDY EXERCISE - Putting It All Together

In the following Study Exercise you are going to have your

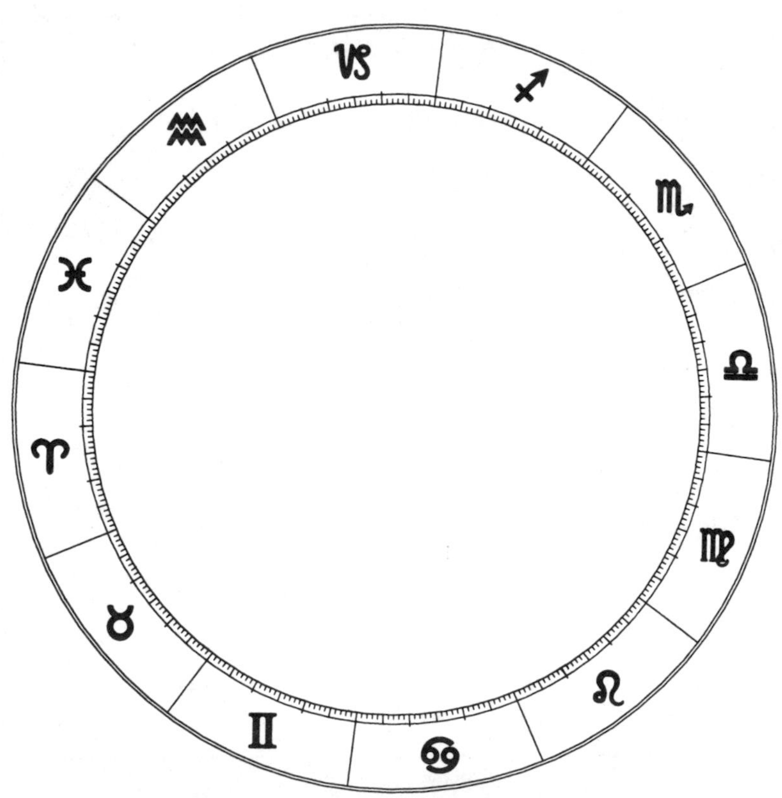

first chance to put all the pieces together. Prediction is an art. You can rely on your intuition for viewing the whole after studying each important piece.

<u>Step #1</u>

Using the Ephemeris in the back of the book, look up the location for all Slow Moving Planets on today's date. Mark their locations in the Zodiac Wheel provided. (Note: If you have purchased "The Works," simply transcribe all recent past and forthcoming Aspects into the Study Form in chronological order. Include House Rulership information.)

STUDY FORM - Putting It All Together

Month/Year	Aspect/RH	Comment
__________	__________	
__________	__________	
__________	__________	
__________	__________	
__________	__________	
__________	__________	
__________	__________	
__________	__________	
__________	__________	
__________	__________	
__________	__________	
__________	__________	
__________	__________	
__________	__________	
__________	__________	
__________	__________	
__________	__________	

Step #2

Looking at your Natal Chart, note possible Aspects that could be made by the Slow Moving Planets you noted in the Zodiac Wheel. Make a note by each Transit regarding the possible forthcoming and past Aspect. Also, note what the exact position of the Transiting Planet must be in order for the Aspect to become Exact.

Step #3

Using the Ephemeris in the back of the book, look up the dates the Aspects will become Exact. Notate the date next to the Aspect on the Zodiac Wheel.

Step #4

Review the data on your Zodiac wheel and transcribe this information into chronological order in your Study Form. Next to your Natal Planet, note the House it Rules.

Predicting - Putting It All Together

Using Appendix Two to determine House matters, focus on events resulting from Jupiter and Saturn. Then, use the Aspects formed by the remaining Slow Moving Planets to determine the conditions under which the events will manifest. Once you have reviewed your current Transits in this Study Exercise, examine any other two periods of your life. I suggest you study at least one commitment time and any other time you feel you had undergone major changes.

FINAL NOTE

As your studies progress, you may find it easier to write down the location of Transiting Planets on your Natal Chart after making copies. Viewing the Transits this way gives you the whole prospective at a glance. For determining the specific order of events and making predictions, you can list the Aspects being made, along with the dates they become Exact, on a separate piece of paper.

STUDY FORM - Putting It All Together

Month/Year	Aspect/RH	Comment
________	________	
________	________	
________	________	
________	________	
________	________	
________	________	
________	________	
________	________	
________	________	
________	________	
________	________	
________	________	
________	________	
________	________	
________	________	
________	________	
________	________	
________	________	
________	________	
________	________	
________	________	
________	________	
________	________	
________	________	

STUDY FORM - Putting It All Together

Month/Year	Aspect/RH	Comment

Chapter Five

CASE STUDY

In order to illustrate the methodology used in determining if two people will marry (or at least have the opportunity to marry) I have created a fictitious person (Fred), situation and birth data. In addition, I matched him (Fred) with a noted single celebrity (Barbra Streisand - using her correct birth data). In order for them to marry each other, Saturn would have to make Soft Aspects to the Rulers of their 7th Houses at about the same time. That in itself is a highly unlikely occurrence. Additionally, from the study we will determine the date of Ms. Streisand's next marriage.

The expectation of this study was that *no* marriage dates would be found. However, a significant Match was found. It warranted further investigation. The further investigation produced conspicuous results.

I am including this study because it serves as an ideal example of the methodology used for determining whether or not two individuals could get married to each other. If that question is answered in the affirmative, then you can determine the approximate date of the marriage, the overall conditions that lead to marriage and continue to predict with accuracy the ultimate fate or challenges of the union.

DEFINITIONS

Match

A Match occurs when Transiting Saturn makes a Soft Aspect to the Ruler of both subjects' 7th House Ruling Planets within a given time period. Thus, if Transit Saturn Trines subject "A's" 7th House Ruler on day one, and Conjuncts subject "B's" 7th House Ruler on day ten; there is a Match.

The Match produces a window of opportunity for marriage between the subjects. This is the key concept and methodology of this study.

Match Differential

The period measured in days between each subjects Match Date.

The Match Differential is used as an index indicating the probability that the event under study could occur between the subjects being studied. The higher the Match Differential the lower the probability that the subjects will marry. The lower the Match Differential, the higher the probability the subjects will marry.

For the purpose of this study, a Match Differential of twenty or more would indicate that the event in question could not occur.

The Delayed Jupiter Effect

If Transit Jupiter makes a Soft Aspect to the 7th House Ruler after Transit Saturn has done so, often it serves to reinforce the commitment cycle, create an additional window and/or create a window of marriage where none had existed before.

Soft Aspects

Theses are Conjunction, Trine and Sextile.

Hard Aspects

These are Square and Opposition.

METHODOLOGY

This study focuses on determining the Astrological possibility of two predetermined individuals marrying each other at some predictable time in the future. The following steps will be performed in sequential order:

1) The Chart Rectification.

2) The 7th House Transit Saturn Search.

Individually, each Chart will be studied to determine the dates in which Transit Saturn makes a Soft Aspects to the Ruler of their 7th House. Thus, there will be two lists of dates; one for the male subject and one for the female subject.

For the purpose of this study the cut off time for the search will be the year 2012.

3) Matching

The dates found resulting from the 7th House Transit Saturn search will be compared. Dates that show a Match Differential of less than 120 will tentatively be considered Matches.

4) Match Study

For each Match found under the parameters of step #3, the following investigation will be done:

All Aspects made by all Slow Moving Planets will be listed starting one year prior to the Match Date.

The purpose of this step is to determine the conditions leading to Transit Saturn's Soft Aspect to their 7th House Ruling Planet. The sensibility here is if one is going to get married, falling in or being in love as well as pleasurable sexual activity should be a part of the process leading to marriage. These are respectively 5th and 8th House matters.

In addition to the above, Step #4 will reveal whether or not the Delayed Jupiter effect is active thus reducing the Match Differential and making the possibility of marriage greater between the subjects.

All Matches having a Match Differential greater than 20 will be automatically eliminated.

5) Conditions

For any Match(es) remaining (Match Differential of 20 of less) the following test will be performed:

Additional conditions will be placed for each Match. These conditions will be based on the sensibility of the Match Date and the subjects' assumed overall condition prior to the Match Date. For example: If a Match is found for the year 2000 and at the time of this study subject "A" is married, a condition would be placed that in order for the predicted event to come about, subject "A" would have to dissolve his current marriage.

Once a condition of sensibility is placed, the subjects' Charts will be analyzed accordingly. Any Matches that can not satisfy the additional conditions will be eliminated.

7) Review
(Note: This was deleted for the 1998 reprint.)

8) Conclusion
Conclusions will be drawn based on the findings of the study.

CHART RECTIFICATION

Streisand

Birth data for Ms. Streisand was supplied by The Rodden Data Bank (11736 - 3rd St, Yucaipa, CA 92399). It is claimed to be per Streisand's birth certificate. All data used for Ms. Streisand's Chart rectification was provided in Randall Riese's biography *Her Name Is Barbra* (C93, Birchlane Press).

Her birth certificate indicates that she was born on April 24, 1942 at 5:04 am EST in Brooklyn, New York. From this information her Birth Chart was calculated (see Chart #7) and her House Rulership determined (see Table #7).

Marriage

She was married to Elliot Gould on 9/13/63 (See Chart #7). An interesting and unusual Aspect shows up in her Chart. Both Jupiter and Saturn are almost exactly 30 degrees (Semi-

Table #7 - House Rulership for Barbra Streisand

House	Sign	Planet Ruler
1	Aries	Mars
2	Taurus	Venus
3	Gemini	Mercury
4	Cancer	Moon
5	Cancer	Moon
6	Leo =Virgo	Sun =Mercury
7	Libra	Venus
8	Scorpio	Pluto
9	Sagittarius	Jupiter
10	Capricorn	Saturn
11	Capricorn	Saturn
12	Aquarius =Pisces	Uranus =Neptune

note: "=" indicates an intercepted Sign fully contained within a House.

Sextile) to the minute in Aspect to the Ruler of her 7th House (Venus). Most often a Semi-Sextile formed by Transit Saturn alone to the Ruler of the Natal 7th House creates conditions that would be considered only favorable for marriage. That is to say, the Semi-Sextile is not an Aspect that in and of itself will manifest marriage. However, with Jupiter in the same favorable configuration, manifestation can occur depending on the over all conditions and the Exactness of both Aspects at any point in time.

The closer the Aspects come to Exact, the more power each Planet has. In Ms. Streisand's case, this force was enough to

CHART #7
Barbra Streisand - Marriage

Barbra
Apr 24 1942 Trop

☉	03° ♉ 33'	-0°00'
☽	10° ♌ 34'	-2°41'
☿	08° ♉ 07'	+0°09'
♀	17° ♓ 35'	-0°23'
♂	28° ♊ 51'	+1°26'
♃	19° ♊ 59'	-0°14'
♄	28° ♉ 12'	-1°47'
♅	28° ♉ 50'	-0°10'
♆℞	27° ♍ 36'	+1°21'
♇	03° ♌ 29'	+4°42'
☊	10° ♍ 50'	-0°00'
Mc	03° ♑ 31'	-0°00'
As	06° ♈ 38'	-0°00'

Sep 13 1963 Trop

☉	20° ♍ 07'	-0°00'
☽	29° ♋ 54'	+0°59'
☿℞	02° ♎ 46'	-4°08'
♀	24° ♍ 04'	+1°23'
♂	00° ♏ 50'	-0°00'
♃℞	17° ♈ 32'	-1°36'
♄℞	17° ♒ 36'	-1°15'
♅	06° ♍ 36'	+0°44'
♆	13° ♏ 32'	+1°44'
♇	12° ♍ 12'	+13°17'
☊	17° ♋ 09'	-0°00'
Mc	09° ♋ 36'	-0°00'
As	08° ♎ 27'	-0°00'

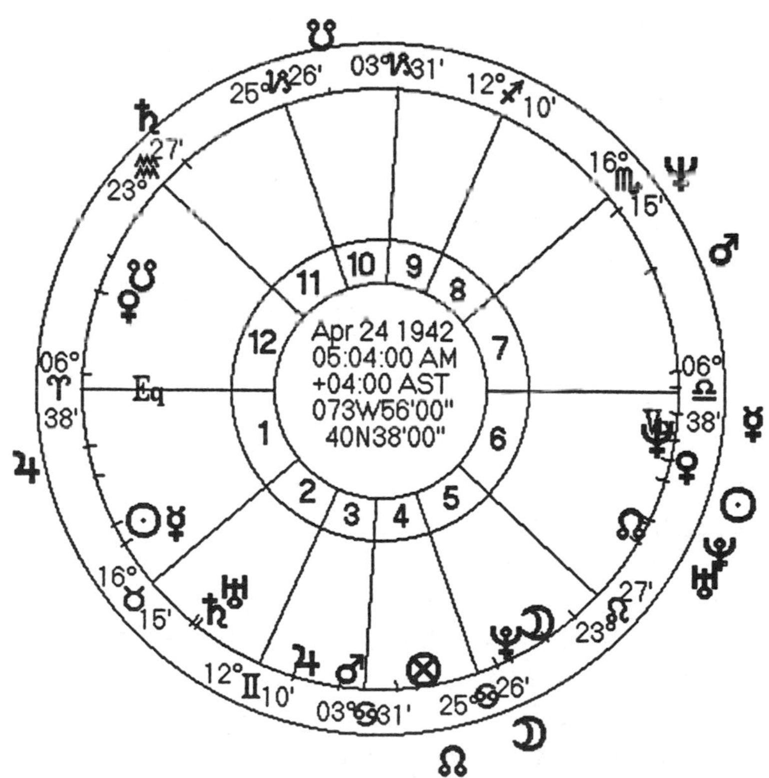

move her into her first major commitment. In addition, it should be noted too that a few months prior to the double Semi-Sextile Aspect made by Transit Jupiter and Saturn, Transit Jupiter made Exact Trines to the Rulers of both her 5th House and 8th House. Given that the 5th House governs love, the 8th House governs sexual activity and Transit Jupiter creates excess under this Aspect, one can predict in retrospect that the events leading to the marriage involved falling in love and having pleasurable physical involvement. Because these events proceeded the Double Semi-Sextile Aspects under investigation, it can be concluded that the they added further strength to her decision to marry at that time under this unique Aspect. It can be speculated that in the absence of this Ideal Marriage Scenario that proceeded her making a commitment (Soft Aspects to her 5th and 8th House Rulers by Transit Jupiter) she probably would not have married under the Double Semi-Sextile Aspect. It was the sum total of events that gave strength to an other wise weak condition for marriage.

Divorce

It was announced publicly on 2/12/69 that she and her husband had separated. (See Chart #8). Looking back in time for Astrological events that would lead to separation, we find that on 9/14/68 Jupiter was in Exact Opposition to the Ruler of her 7th House Ruler. This would indicate that she was having marital challenge outside of her direct control, conditions of endings. But, few Astrologers would consider a single Jupiter Opposition to the Ruler of the 7th House as a causal factor in creating dissolution conditions. However, if one looks progressively at her Chart from the time of marriage to the time of separation one finds that both Uranus as well as Pluto had gone in Opposition to her 7th House Ruler.

CHART #8
Barbra Streisand - Divorce

Barbra
Apr 24 1942 Trop

☉	03° ♉ 33'	- 0°00'
☽	10° ♌ 34'	- 2°41'
☿	08° ♉ 07'	+ 0°09'
♀	17° ♓ 35'	- 0°23'
♂	28° ♊ 51'	+ 1°26'
♃	19° ♊ 59'	- 0°14'
♄	28° ♉ 12'	- 1°47'
♅	28° ♉ 50'	- 0°10'
♆℞	27° ♍ 36'	+ 1°21'
♇	03° ♌ 29'	+ 4°42'
☊	10° ♍ 50'	- 0°00'
Mc	03° ♑ 31'	- 0°00'
As	06° ♈ 38'	- 0°00'

Feb 12 1969 Trop

☉	23° ♒ 45'	- 0°00'
☽	28° ♐ 42'	- 5°10'
☿	00° ♒ 32'	+ 2°03'
♀	09° ♈ 33'	+ 2°21'
♂	24° ♏ 01'	+ 1°16'
♃℞	05° ♎ 13'	+ 1°29'
♄	21° ♈ 09'	- 2°22'
♅℞	03° ♎ 27'	+ 0°46'
♆	28° ♏ 38'	+ 1°42'
♇℞	24° ♍ 33'	+15°52'
☊	02° ♈ 21'	- 0°00'
Mc	12° ♐ 30'	- 0°00'
As	29° ♒ 26'	- 0°00'

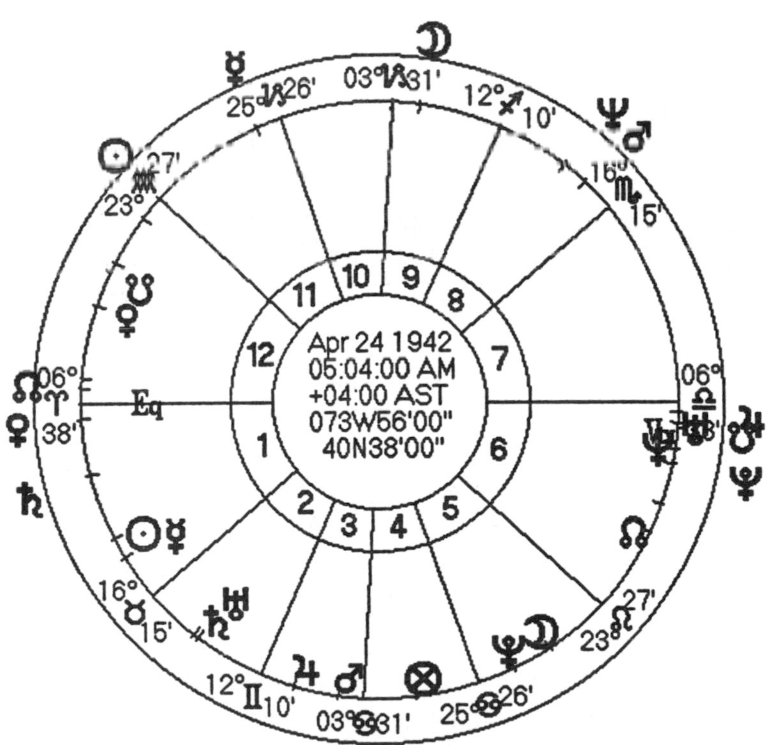

The separation was announced as amicable. They had not necessarily ended the marriage and were quoted as saying that there was love and hope. Looking at her Chart on the day of the public announcement (Chart #8), both Jupiter and Saturn were acting favorably on the Ruler of her 5th House of Love, Mars was moving to Trine to the same Natal Planet and Transit Venus was Conjuncting her Ascendant. From the Astrological prospective, Saturn making Soft Aspects to her Natal 5th House Ruler would create conditions that were favorable for being in love or loving. Transit Mars making a Trine to the same Natal Planet would reinforce this with her personal drive. When she made the public announcement regarding their separation, Transit Venus was passing over her Ascendant indicating her ability to express this most personal matter on a loving basis.

New Love

Her next major love involvement, which ultimately led to a commitment, was to a man named Jon Peters. The first open signs of this relationship showed on Christmas Eve, in 1973. After a Christmas party her friends were quoted as saying that they had never seen her so out of control and so much in love with a man before. Whatever she did or said at the time must have been of an exhibitionist nature in order to generate the series of news media statements that followed. Noting her Chart on that date (See Chart #9) one finds Jupiter in Opposition to the Ruler of her 5th House of Love; love out of her hands. To help her emotional situation further, Transit Pluto was entering a Sextile to the Ruler of her 5th House and Transit Neptune Waning a Trine to the Ruler of her 5th House. Also, Transit Pluto was Conjuncting her 7th House Cusp which brought forward her deepest issues concerning commitment.

Looking to future Aspects on her Chart: Jupiter was about

CHART #9
Barbra Streisand - New Love

Barbra
Apr 24 1942 Trop

☉	03° ♉ 33'	-0°00'
☽	10° ♌ 34'	-2°41'
☿	08° ♉ 07'	+0°09'
♀	17° ♓ 35'	-0°23'
♂	28° ♊ 51'	+1°26'
♃	19° ♊ 59'	-0°14'
♄	28° ♉ 12'	-1°47'
♅	28° ♉ 50'	-0°10'
♆℞	27° ♍ 36'	+1°21'
♇	03° ♌ 29'	+4°42'
☊	10° ♍ 50'	-0°00'
Mc	03° ♑ 31'	-0°00'
As	06° ♈ 38'	-0°00'

Dec 24 1973 Trop

☉	02° ♑ 41'	-0°00'
☽	02° ♑ 46'	+0°23'
☿	23° ♐ 47'	-0°40'
♀	09° ♒ 36'	-0°13'
♂	00° ♉ 06'	+1°00'
♃	12° ♒ 50'	-0°44'
♄℞	01° ♋ 09'	-1°03'
♅	27° ♎ 06'	+0°35'
♆	08° ♐ 05'	+1°33'
♇	06° ♎ 46'	+16°33'
☊	28° ♐ 18'	-0°00'
Mc	23° ♎ 18'	-0°00'
As	01° ♑ 13'	-0°00'

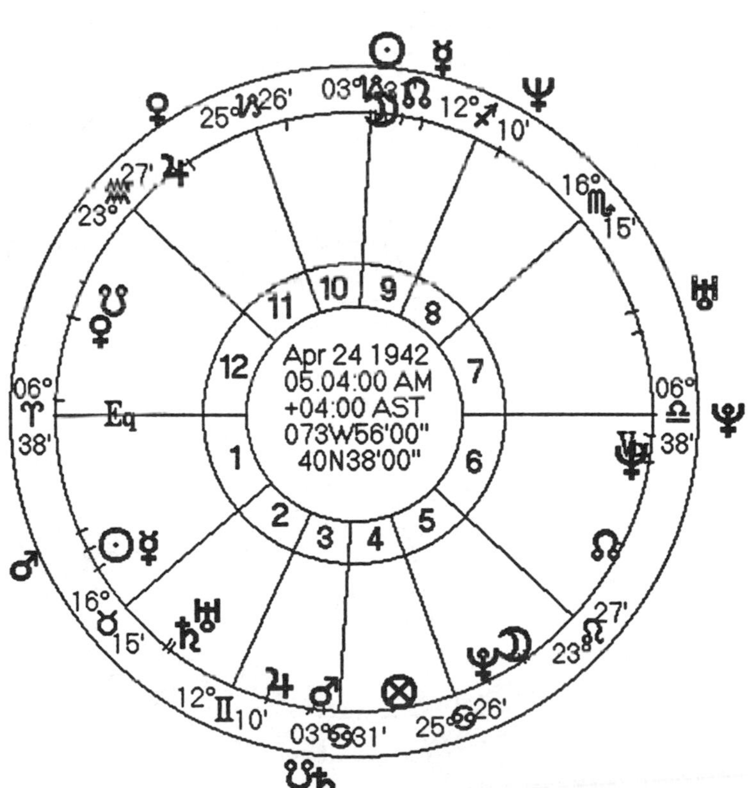

CHART #10
Fred's Natal Chart

☉	21°♋28'	-0°00'
☽	07°♓43'	-3°27'
☿	07°♋24'	-0°04'
♀	14°♌57'	+1°36'
♂	23°♊54'	+0°21'
♃℞	28°♑03'	-0°28'
♄	03°♍36'	+1°37'
♅	02°♋01'	+0°13'
♆	12°♎30'	+1°35'
♇	15°♌25'	+7°38'
☊	21°♈09'	-0°00'
Mc	23°♐09'	-0°00'
As	17°♓39'	-0°00'
Vx	24°♍44'	-0°00'
Eq	21°♓53'	-0°00'
⊗	03°♏54'	-0°00'

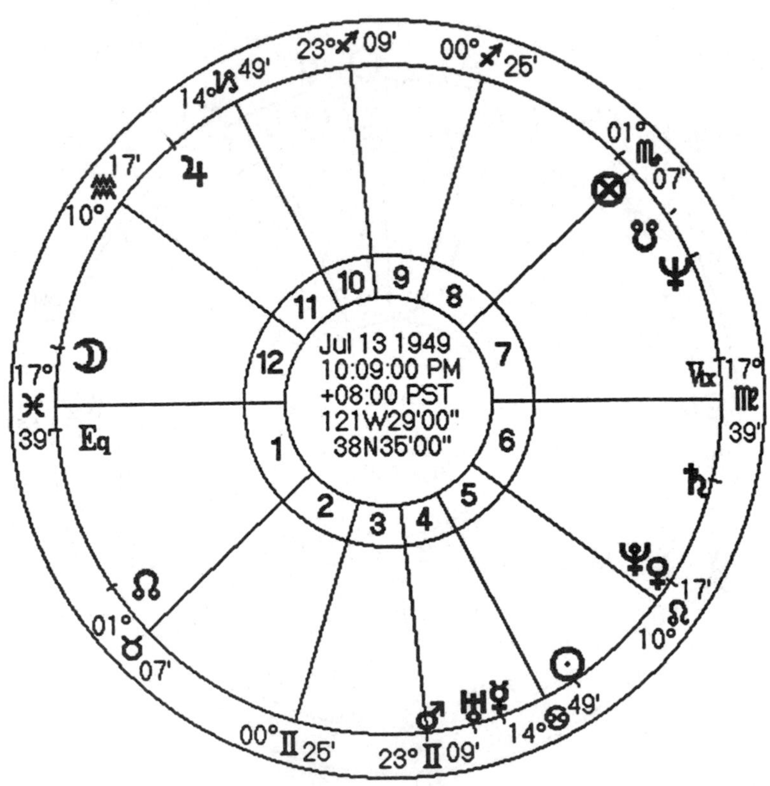

one year away from Conjuncting the Ruler of her 7th House and Saturn was slowly moving to Trine the Ruler of her 7th House. There were no Hard Aspects to the Rulers of her Pertinent Houses (5th, 7th and 8th) by Slow Moving Planets to interfere with the development of this relationship.

The prediction based on these Transits would be that she would make a deep and meaningful commitment to someone and this commitment would last for many years. This is in fact what happened. They lived, loved and worked together for many years.

As a final note in rectifying her Chart it should be mentioned that on March 14, 1994, Transit Uranus made an Exact Conjunction to her 11th House Cusp. Among other things, the 11th House governs large groups of people. Transit Uranus most often brings about extreme, surprising and instantaneous change concerning House issues under this Aspect. The only extreme change possible with regard to her and large groups of people, is standing in front of them and singing. She had not sung publically in over twenty years. About the time this Aspect was Exact, she made the Uranus turnabout and started an international tour.

Given that the source of her Birth Data is considered most reliable and the above rectification coincides with 5th, 7th, 8th and 11th House activities; for the purpose of this study, her Chart has been rectified.

Fred's Chart

Birth Data: July 13, 1949, 10:09 pm PST, Sacramento, CA. His Natal Chart was calculated and is presented in Chart #10. From this, his House Rulerships were determined as shown in Table #8. (In order to conserve space, his Chart rectification will not be included.)

Table #8 - House Rulership for Fred

House	*Sign*	*Ruling Planet(s)*
1	Pisces =Aries	Neptune =Mars
2	Taurus	Venus
3	Gemini	Mercury
4	Gemini	Mercury
5	Cancer	Moon
6	Leo	Sun
7	Capricorn =Libra	Mercury =Venus
8	Scorpio	Pluto
9	Sagittarius	Jupiter
10	Sagittarius	Jupiter
11	Capricorn	Saturn
12	Aquarius	Uranus

Note: "=" indicates an intercepted Sign fully contained within a House.

MATCHING

Using the period starting from the date of this study and ending January 1, 2012, both subjects' Natal Charts were searched for Soft Aspects made by Transit Saturn to the Rulers of their 7th House. (See Table #9.) After a list was compiled for each Chart, the lists were compared. All dates that came within about 120 days of each other were considered tentatively 7th House Matches. Each Match represents a possible window of marriage between the subjects.

Table #9 - Matching

Streisand

	Aspect		DATE
♄	☌	♀	26MAR95
♄	✶	♀	17APRØØ
♄	□	♀	Ø2JUNØ2
♄	△	♀	14JULØ4
♄	☍	♀	21OCTØ8
♄	☍	♀	18MARØ9
♄	☍	♀	13JULØ9

Fred

	Aspect		DATE
♄	△	☿	Ø1APR94
♄	△	☿	23SEP94
♄	△	☿	24DEC94
♄	□	☿	Ø7MAR97
♄	△	♀	Ø8MAY97
♄	△	♀	Ø5NOV97
♄	△	♀	24JAN98
♄	✶	☿	Ø2MAY99
♄	□	♀	Ø9JUL99
♄	□	♀	21OCT99
♄	□	♀	26MARØØ
♄	✶	♀	21SEPØ1
♄	✶	♀	Ø1OCTØ1
♄	✶	♀	12MAYØ2
♄	☌	☿	Ø1AUGØ3
♄	☌	☿	Ø1FEBØ4
♄	☌	☿	11APRØ4
♄	☌	♀	Ø7AUGØ6
♄	✶	☿	13NOVØ7
♄	✶	☿	24JANØ8
♄	✶	☿	28JULØ8
♄	□	☿	27SEP1Ø
♄	✶	♀	Ø5DEC1Ø
♄	✶	♀	2ØMAR11
♄	✶	♀	29AUG11
♄	△	☿	Ø8DEC12

The author does not consider that a 7th House Match separated by 120 days in itself, would lead to marriage between two subjects. This time period was selected in order avoid the possibility of missing Windows of Marriage that were created by the Delayed Jupiter Affect (Soft Jupiter Aspects to the Ruler of the 7th House following Soft Saturn Aspects to the Ruler of the same House. This often creates the conditions that lead to the actual date of marriage.).

Based on the above parameters, the following two Matches were found:

	Streisand	Fred	Match Differential
Match #1-	Mar 26, 1995	Dec 24, 1994	92 Days
Match #2-	Jul 14, 2004	Apr 11, 2004	93 Days

(Note: The dates under each name column show the dates the Aspects become Exact.)

MATCH STUDY

Two Matches were found. Each Match was assigned a reference number. For each Match the following investigation was done: Starting one year prior to the Match Date for each subject and ending a few months after, all Major Aspects made by all Slow Moving Planets in each subjects' Chart were found. Aspects tabulated include Conjunctions made to House Cusps during the period under study.

The sensibility here is twofold: In order to become man and wife, the subjects' Charts should show events leading to the commitment. Most likely these events would be 5th House (love), 8th House (sexuality) and 7th House (commitment) matters. For the purpose of this study, the Aspects being made to these House Rulers would have to be predominately Soft Aspects. The number and type of Aspects will serve as an index to the overall probability of a commitment being made between subjects. The other concern is that the investigation revealed two windows for marriage between the subjects. But in both cases, the Match Differential is so great according to this researcher, neither one of the Matches in themselves would create sufficient conditions that could lead to marriage. This further investigation into Transit Jupiter relative to their 7th House Ruling Planet will reveal the possibility of reducing the Match Differential due to the Delayed Jupiter Effect.

The general guidelines are: If the Match Differential is great and marriage is not supported by events leading to the Match Date, then the Match can be eliminated. On the other hand, if the Match Differential is reasonable and/or can be reduced by the Jupiter Delay Effect and events leading to the Match Date support commitment (positive 5th and 8th House activity), then the Match Date is further supported.

Match #2 (Analysis and Discussion)

Match #2 occurs on July 14 and April 11, 2004. The Match Differential is 93 Days. For the purpose of this study, a Match Differential in excess of 20 will not bring about conditions leading to commitment between two subjects. Thus, Match #2 could be eliminated due to a high Match Differential if further analysis does not show additional supportive material.

The pertinent House activity that proceeds Match #2 by one (See Table #10) starting with Streisand's Chart is as follows: Transit Neptune Opposes the Ruler of her 5th House (her Natal Moon). Pluto Squares the Ruler of her 7th House, Jupiter Opposes the Ruler of her 7th House and finally Saturn

Table #10 - Match #2 Analysis

Fred

♃	✶	♅	05SEP03
♃	☌	♄	12SEP03
♄	□	♆	27SEP03
♃	✶	☿	30SEP03
♃	☍	☽	02OCT03
♄	□	♆	23NOV03
♃	☌	07	06DEC03
♆	△	♆	23JAN04
♄	△	☽	27JAN04
♄	☌	☿	01FEB04
♃	☌	07	
♅	△	♅	08FEB04
♅	☍	♄	07MAR04
♆	☍	♀	06APR04
♄	☌	☿	11APR04
♄	△	☽	16APR04
♄	□	♆	04JUN04
♄	☌	05	22JUN04
♆	☍	♀	28JUN04
♃	☌	07	26JUL04

Streisand

♃	△	☉	12SEP03
♆	☍	☽	27SEP03
♇	□	♀	03OCT03
♃	△	☿	04OCT03
♆	☍	☽	15NOV03
♃	☍	♀	05DEC03
♇	☍	♃	17DEC03
♄	✶	☿	21JAN04
♃	☍	♀	01FEB04
♅	✶	☉	06MAR04
♄	✶	☿	21APR04
♄	△	♀	14JUL04
♇	☍	♃	19JUL04
♃	☍	♀	26JUL04

Trines the Ruler of her 7th House.

Looking at Fred's Chart for Match #2 there are the following pertinent Aspects made: Neptune Opposes the Co-Ruler of his 7th House, Saturn Trines the Ruler of his 5th House, Saturn Conjuncts the Ruler of his 7th House, Jupiter Sextiles the Ruler of his 7th House and Jupiter Conjuncts his 7th house Cusp.

For the purpose of this study, Match #2 will be eliminated as a likely window of marriage between the two subjects for the sum total of following reasons:

1) The Match Differential is 93 days.

2) The Jupiter Delay Effect is not active and thus the Match Differential remains at 93 days.

3) The events leading to the Match Dates are highly mixed thus unable to compensate for the large Match Differential.

Match #1 (Analysis and Discussion)

To proceed into the analysis of Match #1, all Slow Moving Transit Planets making traditional Aspects in each of the subjects Charts are tabulated. (See Table #11 on next page.) This includes Conjunctions being made to their House Cusps.

From these Transit Aspects a most significant and profound finding resulted. Transit Jupiter makes an Exact Trine to the 7th House Co-Ruling Planet in Fred's Chart. This Aspect is Exact on March 15th, 1995 which is eleven days away from Streisand's Match Date. Thus, the Match Differential for Match #1 is 11 as a result of the Delayed Jupiter Effect. A highly significant finding. The Match Differential cannot be over emphasized. It is the exact clockwork behind two individuals of the opposite sex making a commitment. The lower the Match Differential, the higher the possibility they will commit to each other. When a Match differential is below 14, the Predictive Astrologer, aside from being dumbfounded

Table #11 - Match #1 Analysis

Streisand

			DATE
♃	□	☽	Ø6JAN94
♄	□	♄	12JAN94
♄	□	♅	18JAN94
♄	△	♂	
♇	✱	♆	19JAN94
♄	✱	☉	27FEB94
♅	☌	11	14MAR94
♄	✱	☿	Ø8APR94
♇	✱	♆	11APR94
♃	□	☽	23APR94
♃	☍	☿	13MAY94
♅	☌	11	18JUN94
♃	☍	☿	19AUG94
♃	□	☽	Ø5SEP94
♄	✱	☿	13SEP94
♃	☌	Ø8	Ø6OCT94
♃	△	♀	13OCT94
♇	✱	♆	1ØNOV94
♇	☍	♄	25NOV94
♃	✱	♆	28NOV94
♃	☍	♄	3ØNOV94
♃	☍	♅	Ø3DEC94
♇	☍	♅	11DEC94
♃	△	♇	25DEC94
♅	☌	11	3ØDEC94
♄	✱	☿	Ø2JAN95
♃	△	☽	Ø2FEB95
♅	△	♆	Ø6FEB95
♃	☌	Ø9	13FEB95
♅	△	♄	16FEB95
♅	△	♅	Ø1MAR95
♄	☌	♀	26MAR95
♆	☌	11	Ø6APR95
♄	□	♃	17APR95

Table #11 - Continued

Fred

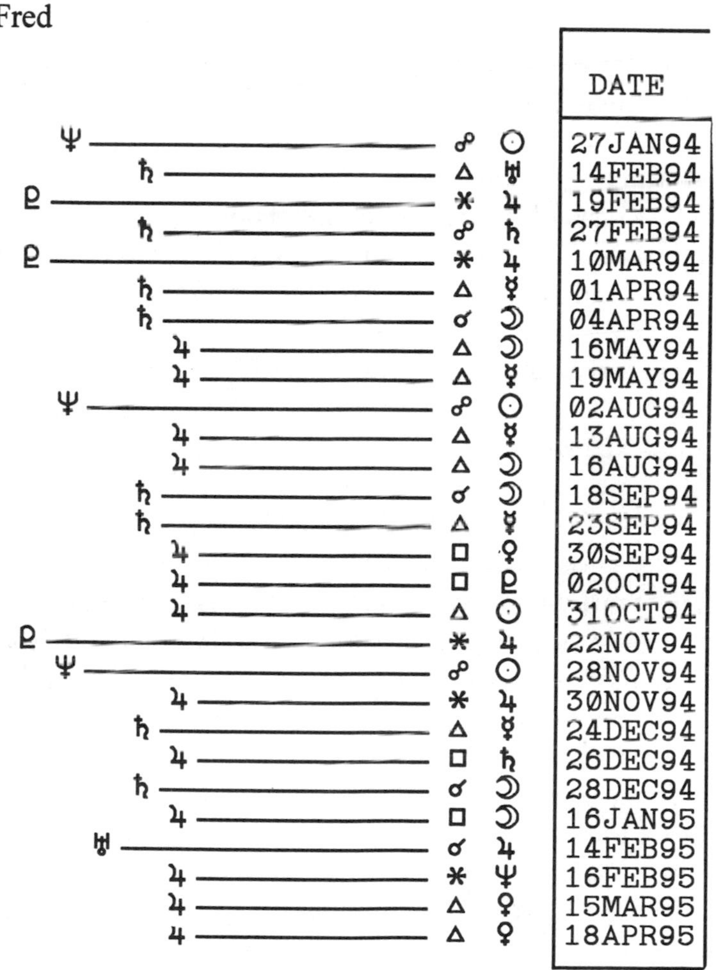

			DATE
♆	☍	☉	27JAN94
♄	△	♅	14FEB94
♇	✶	♃	19FEB94
♄	☍	♄	27FEB94
♇	✶	♃	1ØMAR94
♄	△	☿	Ø1APR94
♄	☌	☽	Ø4APR94
♃	△	☽	16MAY94
♃	△	☿	19MAY94
♆	☍	☉	Ø2AUG94
♃	△	☿	13AUG94
♃	△	☽	16AUG94
♄	☌	☽	18SEP94
♄	△	☿	23SEP94
♃	□	♀	3ØSEP94
♃	□	♇	Ø2OCT94
♃	△	☉	31OCT94
♇	✶	♃	22NOV94
♆	☍	☉	28NOV94
♃	✶	♃	3ØNOV94
♄	△	☿	24DEC94
♃	□	♄	26DEC94
♄	☌	☽	28DEC94
♃	□	☽	16JAN95
♅	☌	♃	14FEB95
♃	✶	♆	16FEB95
♃	△	♀	15MAR95
♃	△	♀	18APR95

by the finding, can predict with certainty, assuming that all other matters are in order, the couple involved will commit to each other on an exclusive basis and on a specific date.

The results of this part of the study are presented in score-keeping format (See Table #12). Viewing the pertinent Aspects in this way gives an instant feel for the overall strength and direction regarding a predicted event.

Ideal Marriage Scenario

Match #1 has a Match Differential of only 11. This is highly significant and indicates a Marriage Window between the two subjects. In addition, both Charts indicate that during the year prior to the Match #1, each subject will fall in love and be active in a very pleasurable way sexually. This activity proceeds Match #1. Thus, the sum total of Match #1 represents the Ideal Marriage Scenario between subjects.

Additional Conditions for Match #1

Unlike a Match Date that is so far into the future that it would be difficult to determine the personal posture of each subject, the exact date for Match #1 is less than one year away. Thus, both subjects lives can be viewed pretty much in their current state for the purpose of posing additional conditions.

These additional conditions will be placed into the Marriage Scenario and must be satisfied in order for the event to occur on Match Date #1. Each condition will be numbered and investigated. If any one of the conditions cannot be reasonably satisfied, Match #1 will be eliminated in its entirety as a possible window of commitment between the subjects.

This final condition procedure is a crucial and important test. From the methodological viewpoint, having the Ideal Marriage Scenario leading to a common window of commitment is a positive and powerful indicator of marriage between

Table #12 - Marriage Scenario Aspects

Subject	House	#	Aspect	Transit Planet
Streisand	5th	3	Squares	Jupiter
	5th	2	Trines	Jupiter
	8th	1	Trine	Jupiter
	7th	1	Trine	Jupiter
	7th	1	Conjunction	Saturn
Fred	5th	2	Trines	Jupiter
	5th	1	Square	Jupiter
	5th	3	Conjunction	Saturn
	8th	1	Square	Jupiter
	8th	1	Trine	Jupiter
	7th	2	Trine	Jupiter
	7th	3	Trine	Saturn
	=7th	1	Trine	Jupiter

(Note: "= " indicates House Co-Ruler.)

The category "#" above indicates the number of times particular as Aspect is made or becomes Exact.

two subjects. These final tests revolve around conditions that absolutely must come to about in order for the two subjects to follow this path *together* and enter the commitment window *hand and hand.*

Condition #1: Shared Asset Condition

Given the current financial status of the male subject and the female subject, financially a marriage would be in favor of the male. This is an 8th House (shared assets) matter. To understand the nature of the condition more clearly it should be understood the female subject is reported to have personal assets in excess of 100 million dollars plus a continued income generated from royalties, performances, etc. On the other hand, the male subject would be considered financially successful but normal in that regard.

To become man and wife there would be extreme and excessive changes regarding 8th House matters. The two Transit Planets we have defined by "extreme and excessive" are Jupiter (excess) and Uranus (extreme). Thus, the specific, clearly defined and only Astrological events that will satisfy condition #1 are: Transiting Uranus and Jupiter would have to be directly involved with the Ruling Planet of both their 8th Houses and/or making Transit activity to their 8th House Cusp.

Examining their Charts on the Match Date #1 (See Charts 11 and 12) the following was found: In Fred's Chart, Jupiter is Trining the Ruler of his 8th House. At the same time Jupiter Trines the Ruler of his 8th House, Venus stands in Opposition to the Ruler of his 8th House, Mars Conjuncts the Ruler of his 8th House and Saturn makes a Quincunx to the Ruler of his 8th House. From the interpretive perspective with regard to this 8th House activity, the following could be concluded assuming the event under study occurred: He would in fact immediately benefit financially from his marriage as indicated by the Jupiter Trine to his Natal Pluto Ruling his 8th House of Shared Assets. The financial benefit will come in such a way that does not require any effort on his part at the time of manifestation and will be in excess. The financial benefit will be triggered by a loving nature outside of his direct control due to the Venus Opposition. Mars Conjuncting his Natal Pluto at the same time would indicate that the event would directly engage his drive and territorial forces. Meanwhile, Saturn forms a Quincunx (150 degrees) to his Natal Pluto, which would indicate that tension could result from some sort of restriction concerning the shared asset activity.

This condition concerning shared assets is satisfied in the male subject's Chart in a profound manner. However, in order for Condition #1 to be satisfied, both subjects' 8th Houses must have extreme and/or excess Astrological conditions. Otherwise, based on sound premise, the predicted event could absolutely not occur. Thus, we must look to the female subject's Chart. (Note: It should be emphasized that the purpose of this study is not to determine if the event will occur. The purpose is to determine if it *could* occur.)

Transit Uranus is included as a part of Condition #1. This Transit was not found in the male subjects Chart. Therefore, to satisfy Condition #1 Transit Uranus must appear in the female's Chart active on the date of Match #1.

The Ruler of the female subject's 8th House is Pluto. Looking at the Transits on Match Date #1, one finds the following (see Chart #12): Transit Uranus is in Opposition with a 3 1/2 degree waning Orb, while Transit Pluto is making a Trine to her Natal Pluto with a Waning Orb of 3 degrees. The Orbs could be considered marginal in so far as bringing about an event is concerned. But given the energy of both Slow Moving Planets plus the fact that a few days prior to Match #1 the drive force of Transit Mars makes a direct Conjunct to her Natal Pluto thus activating, triggering or causing an initial re-

CHART #11
Fred's Chart for Match Date #1

☉	21°♋28'	-0°00'
☽	07°♓43'	-3°27'
☿	07°♋24'	-0°04'
♀	14°♌57'	+1°36'
♂	23°♊54'	+0°21'
♃℞	28°♑03'	-0°28'
♄	03°♍36'	+1°37'
♅	02°♋01'	+0°13'
♆	12°♎30'	+1°35'
♇	15°♌25'	+7°38'
☊	21°♈09'	-0°00'
Mc	23°♐09'	-0°00'
As	17°♓39'	-0°00'

Mar 15 1995 Trop		
☉	24°♓54'	-0°00'
☽	10°♍47'	-4°15'
☿	01°♓31'	-1°58'
♀	15°♒23'	+0°04'
♂℞	13°♌39'	+3°46'
♃	14°♐58'	+0°48'
♄	16°♓13'	-1°46'
♅	29°♑27'	-0°31'
♆	25°♑04'	+0°33'
♇℞	00°♐35'	+13°45'
☊	07°♏51'	-0°00'
Mc	10°♉34'	-0°00'
As	18°♌21'	-0°00'

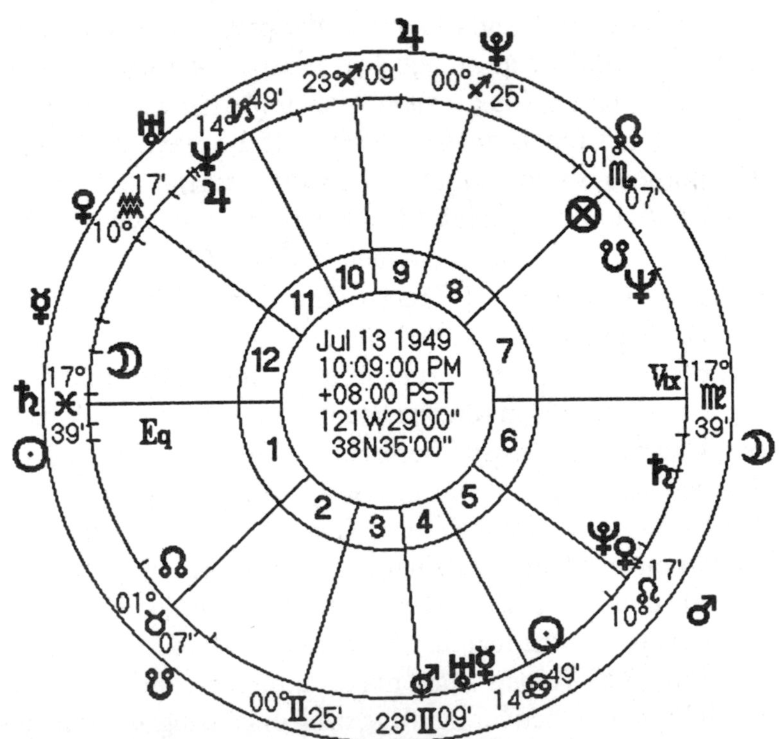

CHART #12
Barbra Streisand's Chart for Match Date #1

☉	03°♉33'	-0°00'
☽	10°♌34'	-2°41'
☿	08°♉07'	+0°09'
♀	17°♓35'	-0°23'
♂	28°♊51'	+1°26'
♃	19°♊59'	-0°14'
♄	28°♉12'	-1°47'
♅	28°♉50'	-0°10'
♆℞	27°♍38'	+1°21'
♇	03°♌29'	+4°42'
☊	10°♍50'	-0°00'
Mc	03°♑31'	-0°00'
As	06°♈38'	-0°00'

Mar 26 1995 Trop		
☉	05°♈49'	-0°00'
☽	15°♒52'	+5°08'
☿	18°♓48'	-2°19'
♀	28°♒30'	-0°33'
♂	13°♌12'	+3°20'
♃	15°♐20'	+0°49'
♄	17°♓33'	-1°47'
♅	29°♑50'	-0°31'
♆	25°♑17'	+0°33'
♇℞	00°♐28'	+13°49'
☊	07°♏16'	-0°00'
Mc	21°♉25'	-0°00'
As	26°♌59'	-0°00'

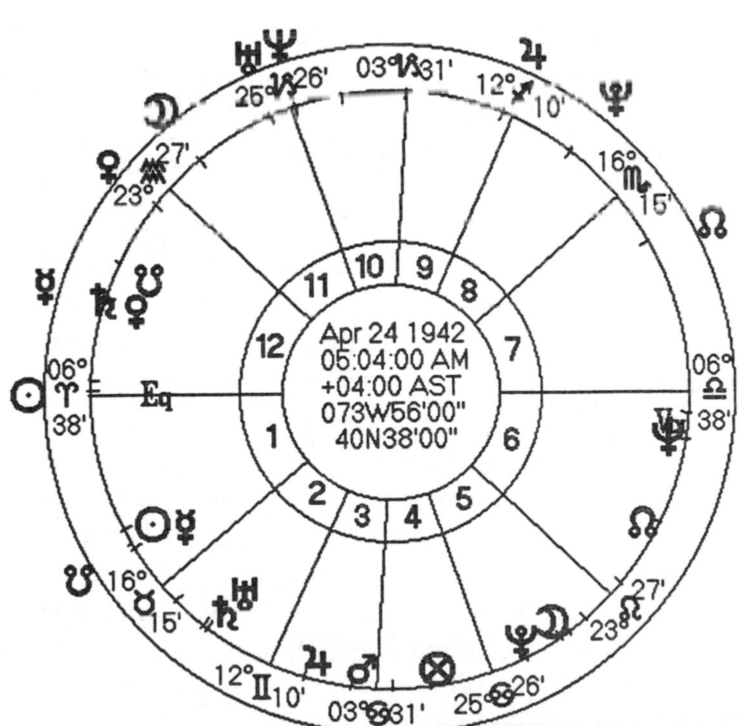

lease and because the Planets involved are Slow Moving, this event would become meaningful and continue over many years. The power of Transit Uranus coupled with Pluto would indicate not only an extreme shared asset situation but it is indicative of a critical extravagant transformation focused on her deepest personal unconsciousness, which will be active over the several years of commitment.

The findings thus far make sence from the prospective that most often Transit Uranus involvement with the 8th House Ruler is indicative of giving. Transit Jupiter involved with the 8th House usually indicates receiving. The scenario set up under Condition #1 suggests that the female subject will give and the male subject receive. The finding is that Transit Uranus in involved with the female subject's 8th House, thus placing her in the giving posture and the male's Transits place him in the receiving posture regarding shared assets.

Both Charts clearly satisfy the overall requirements of extreme (by definition a Uranus Transit) and excess (a Jupiter Transit) acting on their 8th Houses on Match Date #1.

Condition #2- Short Distance Travel Condition

Because the subjects live in different cities, an additional requirement can placed on Match Date #1. In order for them to get to know each other, one or both of them would have to either move their place of residence or travel back and forth. This could require a significant amount of short distance travel. Also, if they did make a commitment, one of them may move as they currently live in different cities. The condition of going back and forth comes under the Rulership of the 3rd House (short distance travel). To satisfy this condition, Jupiter, which manifests excess or abundance, would have to make Traditional Aspects to the Ruling Planet of one of their 3rd Houses or 3rd House Cusp.

The Ruling Planet for Fred's 3rd House is Mercury which is the same Planet Ruling his 7th House. Thus, all Aspects made to his 7th House Ruling Planet listed in Table #11 are applicable to this new condition. Looking at Table #11, one sees that their is significant Saturn and Jupiter activity satisfying the condition of short distance travel. It should also be noted that Mercury governs his 4th House of Home as well, thus satisfying the condition of having to move in order for the event under investigation to come about on the Match Date #1.

In Streisand's Chart the Transits would indicate that she could also move, but there is no indication of short distance travel.

The prediction here could be that if the event under study did in fact come about, it would involve Fred going back and forth to her and at the time of commitment, they would buy a new home which neither one had previously lived in.

The above series of Aspects satisfy Condition #2.

Condition #3 - The Fame Condition

One of the obvious conditions that can be set revolves around Streisand's fame. Because Fred is normal with that regard, marriage to her would bring instant fame by association. A condition can be set that in order for the event to occur on Match Date #1, the male subject's Chart would have to indicate immediate and extreme fame. It would have to be immediate because the event date is close in time and would have to be extreme because the process of moving from nonrecognition by the masses to recognition would be considered an extreme change.

Although interaction with large groups of people is considered an 11th House matter, fame itself is generally considered a 10th House matter by the majority of Astrologers. The condition of immediate and extreme could only be satisfied by Transit Uranus. So, the new condition of immediate fame can only be satisfied if Transit Uranus were making a traditional Aspect to either the Ruler of the male subject's 10th House or an Aspect to his 10th House Cusp.

Looking at his Chart on the Match Date #1 (Chart #11) one finds that Transit Uranus is in Conjunction to his Natal Jupiter, which governs his 10th House activities. This satisfies Condition #3 in a striking manner.

Conditions - Discussion

All conditions were satisfied. That in itself lends further credence to the investigation. If one of the above conditions could not be satisfied, the only conclusion that could be reached is the event under study could not come about on Match Date #1. This would eliminate Match #1 and in as much as it is the only Match, the conclusion of the study would indicate that the two subjects would never make a commitment between them. This however is not the case.

It should be noted that not only were all three conditions satisfied but the Transit Aspects involved in satisfying them were all Soft Aspects. The Soft Aspects would indicate that not only could these events occur but if they did they would all appear naturally and harmoniously. Things would just fall in place. This is highly significant and lends further evidence to the overall linear path leading to Match Date #1.

CONCLUSION

If the event foretold in the male subject's vision were prophecy, he and Ms. Barbra Joan Streisand will be married in

March of 1995. The one exception to this date is mid-December 1995 when Transiting Saturn makes a Waxing Station 24 minutes (about 1/2 degree) from Venus, Ms. Streisand's 7th House Ruler. A final Station this close to the 7th House Ruler, even though Saturn continues forward without making an Exact Conjunction to the 7th Houses Ruler, often can Trigger the final event (in this case, permanent commitment/marriage). A similar situation exists in Fred's Chart as well. Thus, mid-December 1995 is a highly possible date as well as March 1995. These dates represent the only times for them to marry each other and thus fulfill Fred's vision as prophecy. These are the exclusive and only windows of marriage that exist between them. If they don't marry each other on these specific dates, they will never be married to each other. However, no matter what happens between them, they will both be married/committed by these dates.

SECOND PRINTING UPDATE (April 24, 1998)

Since the writing of this book in 1994, as predicted in the "Case Study," the following has occurred. Barbra Streisand and James Broland were introduced by a mutual friend at a private dinner party in 1995. Several months thereafter (July 4, 1996), Jim moved into her Malibu estate. Then, during the July 4th 1998 holiday (shortly after Transiting Jupiter conjuncted her 7th House Ruling Planet Venus) they were married.

Let's look to the future of this relationship. This is *his* third marriage and throughout 1999 Transiting Saturn is going to be Squaring his ***Seventh*** House Ruling Planet. Can you predict the conditions of the marriage for next year? It should be obvious. It may help you to add to *his* astrological configuration the Aspects in *her* 1999 Chart: Transiting Saturn will be Squaring both the Rulers of her ***Eighth*** and ***Fifth*** House.

PREDICTIONS FOR 1999 & 2000

Bill Clinton

Tragically, Clinton will not finish his office of president. It will end due to either resignation, impeachment, or death (natural causes or assassination). This event could occur any time between October 1998 and December 1999. The most likely time periods for the event are October 1998 through February 1999 (mid January 1999 being the most likely month in this time span) and September 1999 through October 1999.

The U.S. Economy

The American economy (on a domestic and international level) will take major and unexpected shifts in 1999. Ultimately this will result in a favorable national economic restructuring. It will culminate in America forming new and more powerful world alliances throughout 1999 and 2000.

Appendix One

THE PLANETS

The Planets are divided into two groups: Slow Moving and Fast Moving. For the purpose of prediction, the Fast Moving Planets act to trigger (see page 80) the manifestation of events predicted through the use of Slow Moving Planets such as Saturn. In doing so, they can dictate the way in which a manifestation is released. For example Venus acting as a trigger could indicate the release of an event through a loving nature.

The times shown for "Around the Zodiac" and "In One Sign" are approximate.

FAST MOVING PLANETS

MOON
Around the Zodiac in 1 month
In one Sign for 2 1/2 days
Alchemy Element is Silver
Essence Power is Feelings
Nature and Focus of the Moon:
Feelings
Emotions
The mothering, nurturing or feminine side

SUN
Around the Zodiac in 1 year
In one Sign for 30 days
Alchemy Element is Gold
Essence Power is Vitality
Nature and Focus of the Sun:
Vitality
Outward personality
Essence of the soul's expression on Earth
The basic expression of to be

MERCURY
Around the Zodiac in 88 days
In one Sign for 7 1/2 days
Alchemy Element is Quicksilver
Essence Power is Logic
Nature and Focus of Mercury:
Logic
Mechanical things
The logical end of anything requiring logic
The mail

Finite reasoning
Appointments
Automobiles
Computers

Mercury governs the ability to think, speak and reason. Also, anything that operates on a logical basis or is relied upon to be logical including mechanical things.

It governs the ability to identify important information, process this and relate it through words. For prediction: As a Natal Planet, it usually means two. For example when predicting marriage, if Mercury Rules the 7th House, when commitment comes about it could involve a choice between two people.

VENUS

Around the Zodiac in 225 days
In one Sign for 19 days
Alchemy Element is Copper
Essence Power is Love
Nature and focus of Venus:
Love
Beauty
Music
Art
Values
Theatrics

MARS

Around the Zodiac in 2 years
In one Sign for 2 months
Alchemy Element is Iron
Essence Power is Drive
Nature and focus of Mars:

Basic drive force
Territory
Physical sexual energy
Courage
Transiting mars destroys that which blocks the spiritual path

SLOW MOVING PLANETS

JUPITER
Around the Zodiac in 12 years
In one Sign for one year
Alchemy Element is Tin
Essence Power is Expansion
Nature and focus of Jupiter:
Returns: In prediction, it indicates returns from the past.
Physical manifester
As a Transit, it expands one's ego recognized limitations
Spiritual development
Traditionally considered the luckiest Planet
Expansion of consciousness
Excess
Abundance
Education
Tests
Expansion

Returns: In prediction, it indicates returns from the past. For example: Jupiter Conjuncting the 5th House Ruling Planet could indicate the return of an old love or anything 5th House related.

SATURN
Around the Zodiac in 29 years

In one sign for 2.5 years
Alchemy Element is Lead
Essence power is Restriction
Nature and Focus of Saturn energy:
Physical manifester
Restriction

URANUS
Around the Zodiac in 84 years
In one sign for 7 years
Higher Octave of Mercury
Essence Power is a Catalyst
Nature and Focus of Uranus:
Speeds up existing conditions
Instant
Extremes
Sudden change
Surprises
Identity
Psychic ability
Instant knowingness/Intuition
Unconventionalism
Higher mind
Innovation
Genius
Science fiction
Accelerates a situation

NEPTUNE
Around the Zodiac in 165 years
In one Sign for 14 years
Higher octave of Venus
Essence Power is a Solvent

Nature and focus of Neptune:
Transcendence beyond the material plane
Deception
Infidelity
Alcoholism
Creative ability in the literary, poetic and music fields.
Theatrics
Intuition, clairvoyance, contact with higher invisible worlds
Illusion
Dissolves what Saturn built
Reaches the sublime heights or the lowest depths
Rules the astral plane, the next dimension
Closely associated with imagination where Uranus is more associated with intuition

PLUTO
Around Zodiac in 248 years
In one Sign for 20 years
Higher octave of Mars
Essence Power is Transformation
Nature and Focus of Pluto:
Deep inside stuff - Usually below consciousness mind
Death and regeneration
Like a volcano it builds up below surface and erupts
Nicknames - Lord of the Underworld, God of Hell, and God of Death
Deepest fears and highest sence of purpose
Death/Rebirth
Obsessiveness
Need to get at the bottom of the matter

Appendix Two

THE HOUSES

Every House has an Essence from which all else is derived. After reading through the Houses, by association you should be able to correctly place items which may not be listed here. For example "the mail": It is a form of communication involving writing. Communication and writing are always 3rd House matters.

1st HOUSE
Essence is The Mask
Nickname: The Mask
House Rulership:
Who you believe yourself to be
How one has chosen to convey them selves as an individual in this life
How you have chosen to project yourself in this life
The face
The general condition and energy level of the aura
Your mask
Your aura
Overall energy condition
Physical body as a reflection of the energy body
Outlook on life

2nd HOUSE
Essence is Self-Esteem
Nickname: House of Money
House Rulership:
How you feel about who you believe yourself to be (Whereas the 1st House governs who you believe yourself to be)
Disposable cash
Values
Personal possessions
Movable possessions
Personal resources
What one likes

3rd HOUSE
Essence is Communication
House Rulership:
The environment closest to current consciousness that requires little personal inward change to become aware of
Also, the physical environment closest to where you are
The local community
The immediate environment
Siblings
Early education
Early environment
Short trips
Teachers
Early childhood environment
Written agreements and legal documents
Your ability to relate to your environment
The mail
Writing
Communications
Computers
Automobiles
Letters

4th HOUSE
Essence is Roots
Nickname: House of Home
House Rulership:
Home
Mother
Soul
Real estate, property or land

5th HOUSE
Essence is Creation
Nickname: House of Love
House Rulership:
Love - who you love and who loves you
Pleasurable activities
Fun
Children
Your children
Hobbies
Dating
Dancing
Music
Creative self-expression
Speculation/gambeling
Entertainment or theatrical endeavors
Honeymoon
Twins (if being a twin is a fun thing)

6th HOUSE
Essence is Charity
NickName: House of Health
House Rulership:
Health
Service - who/how you serve and who/how you are served by others without motive for reward
Work - conditions at your work and relationship with work associates
Cashiers, waiters, waitresses
The practice of healing arts

People in life that may come forward to serve you. For example: While shopping, a helpful person or a person giving directions while traveling.

7th HOUSE
Essence is One-on-One Relationships
NickName: House of Marriage
House Rulership:
Committed one-on-one relationships
Marriage
Partnerships: business, social or otherwise.

8th HOUSE
Essence is Transformation
Nickname: House of Sex
House Rulership:
Transformation
Shared assets
Sex
Death - because transformation requires death of something
Birth - because transformation results in something new
Inheritances
Taxes
Credit

9th HOUSE
Essence is Expansion.
House Rulership:
Expansion of consciousness
Education
Distant travel
Spirituality
Spiritual vision
Schools
Tests
Introductions
The release of an author's work
Publishing

10th HOUSE
Essence is Earthly Purpose
Nickname: House of Career
House Rulership:
Career
Social standing and power
Fame
Recognition

11th HOUSE
Essence is Vision
Nicknname: House of Friends
House Rulership:
Goals
Hopes, dreams and wishes
Friends
Large groups of people
Personal hopes and wishes

12th HOUSE
Essence is The Personal Unconscious
Nickname: House of Karma
House Rulership:
Habits
Personal psychological makeup
Confining institutions of all kinds such as hospitals, monasteries and prisons
Karma
What you bring forward into this life from your past lives and the past from this life on an unconsciousness level

ASCENDANT

Depending on the House system used, the Ascendant (indicated on Charts as:"Asc.") may or may not be on the Cusp of the 1st House. With the Placidus Houses System, it is always the same as the 1st House Cusp. I recommend that you use the Placidus House System.

The Ascendant is tied to how your will is directed to your personal life. (Soft Aspects made to your Asc. by Transiting Jupiter are the best times for visualizing your desires as they are more likely to manifest under this Aspect.) It includes such matters as: life style; the will; one's expression of their will with regard to their life style; how you view the world.

NODES

The Nodes (☋ South Node / ☊ North Node) represent an Arc made by the Moon. They express a polarity. The South Node indicates areas from past lives that are emphasized and the North Node indicates an area that should be explored in this life.

For predicting, the South Node can bring in past life issues.

Appendix Three

TERMINOLOGY

ARABIC PARTS

A point on the Zodiac whose position is derived from a combination of other points. See "Part of Fortune."

ASCENDANT (ASC.)

A point of intersection of the Ecliptic and horizon nearest the East point. The degree of the Zodiac of this point at the moment of birth usually marks the Cusp of the 1st House in most House systems. The Sign of the Ascendant is commonly called the Rising Sign.

ASPECTS

The angular separation of two planets relative to Earth, measured in Degrees.

BIRTH CHART

Astrological information calculated according to one's Birth Data. Also referred to as Birth Stamp and Natal Chart.

BIRTH DATA

The month, date, year, city and time of birth. This is used for calculating the Natal or Birth Chart.

CO-RULING PLANET

The Planet that Rules a Co-Ruling Sign.

CO-RULING SIGN

A Sign contained completely within a House.

CUSP

The point of intersection by a House Line in the Zodiac.

DIRECT

The "normal" direction of Planets from our perspective here on Earth.

ECLIPTIC

The apparent path or plane of all Planets through the Zodiac.

EPHEMERIS

A book containing a listing of Planet locations at specified time intervals.

GEOCENTRIC PERSPECTIVE

Viewing the heavens with Earth as the center. This is the perspective used by Astrologers.

GRAND CONJUNCTION

A Grand Conjunction occurs when Transit Jupiter and Transit Saturn fROm a Conjunction.

HIT

When an Aspect becomes Exact, it is considered to be a Hit.

HOT POINT

Any point on the Natal Chart where activity on some level will occur as a result of a Transit.

HOUSES

Division of the Natal Chart into twelve sections. There are many House Systems, each one having valid claims for its use. The House System recommended by this book is the Placidus system and is the most popular system today.

HOUSE CUSP

The point of intersection in the Zodiac by a House Line.

HOUSE LINE

The lines used to divide the various twelve Houses.

HOUSE RULERSHIP

Matters that are Ruled by a particular House.

INTERCEPTED SIGN

A Sign contained completely within a House.

MAJOR ASPECT

The Conjunction, Sextile, Trine, Square and/or Opposition.

NATAL CHART

Same as Birth Chart.

NATAL PLANET

Referring to a Planet contained within a Birth Chart.

NODES

This usually refers to the Moon's Nodes. It is the axis where the orbital plane of the Moon intersects the plane of the Ecliptic.

ORB

A distance measured in degrees before and after an Aspect becomes Exact.

PART OF FORTUNE - ⊗

This position on the Birth Chart is as distant from the Ascendant as the Moon is from the Sun (Ascendant + Moon - Sun). It is a Hot Spot for activity according to the House in which it is contained and the Aspect being made.

PLANET

In Astrology the Sun and Moon are considered Planets along with Venus, Mars, Mercury, Jupiter, Saturn, Uranus, Neptune and Pluto.

RISING SIGN

The Sign in the Zodiac intersected by the Ascendant.

SIGNS

The twelve divisions of the Zodiac according to Signs.

RETROGRADE

From our perspective on Earth, Planets occasionally appear to move backward in the sky. When they do, they are said to by in Retrograde.

RULING PLANET

The Planet that Rules the Sign intersected by a House Line.

RULING SIGN

The Sign that is intersected by a House Line.

TRANSITING PLANETS

The motion and/or position of Planets in the heavens as opposed to their fixed location on a Birth Chart.

WANING ORB

An Orb created before an Aspect has become Exact. Unless the Transiting Planet is retrograde at the time, the size of the orb is decreasing.

WAXING ORB

An Orb created after an Aspect has become Exact. Unless the Transiting Planet has gone retrograde, the size of the Orb is increasing.

ZODIAC

The division of the twelve Astrological Signs surrounding Earth used to plot locations in the heavens.

Appendix Four

STUDY EXERCISE ANSWERS

Page 12 - Zodiac Notation

1) 5°♋57′ 2) 25°♉37′ 3) 22°♋27′ 4) 22°♑17′
5) 3°♎1′ 6) 0°♏19′

Page 13 - Ploting Locations in the Zodiac

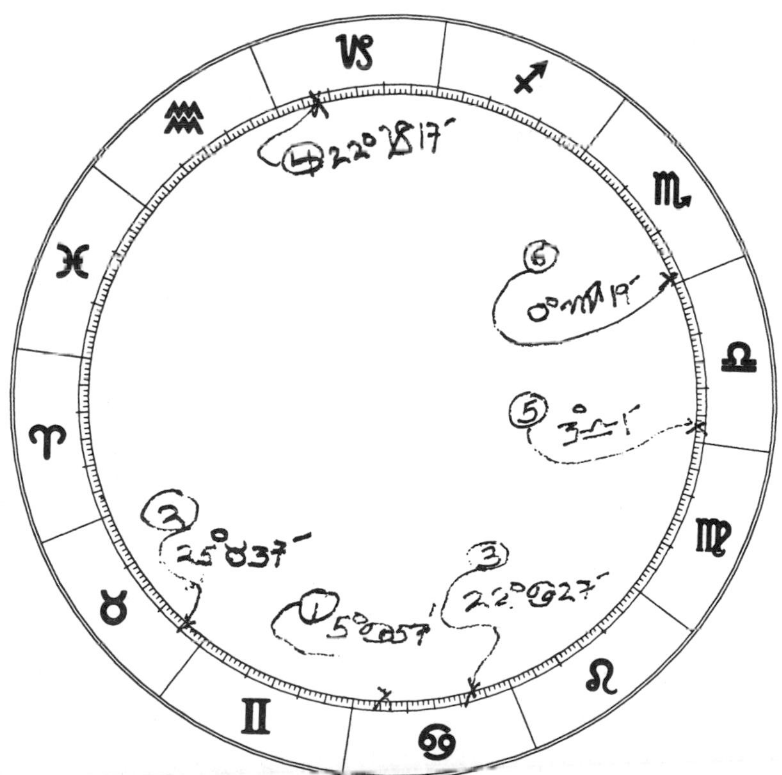

Page 18 - House Sign Rulership
1) Aries 2) Taurus 3) Gemini 4) Cancer 5) Cancer
6) Leo 7) Libra 8) Scorpio 9) Sagittarius 10) Capricorn
11) Capricorn 12) Aquarius

Page 20 - House Planet Rulership
1) Mars 2) Venus 3) Mercury 4) Moon 5) Moon
6) Sun =Mercury 7) Venus 8) Pluto 9) Jupiter
10) Saturn 11) Saturn 12) Uranus =Neptune

Page 22 and 23 - Using the Ephemeris
a) 7 degrees in Aries
b) 17 degrees in Capricorn
c) 14 degrees in Sagittarius
d) 30 degrees in Leo
e) 7 degrees Scorpio
f) 13 degrees Aquarius

Page 28 - Locating Aspects

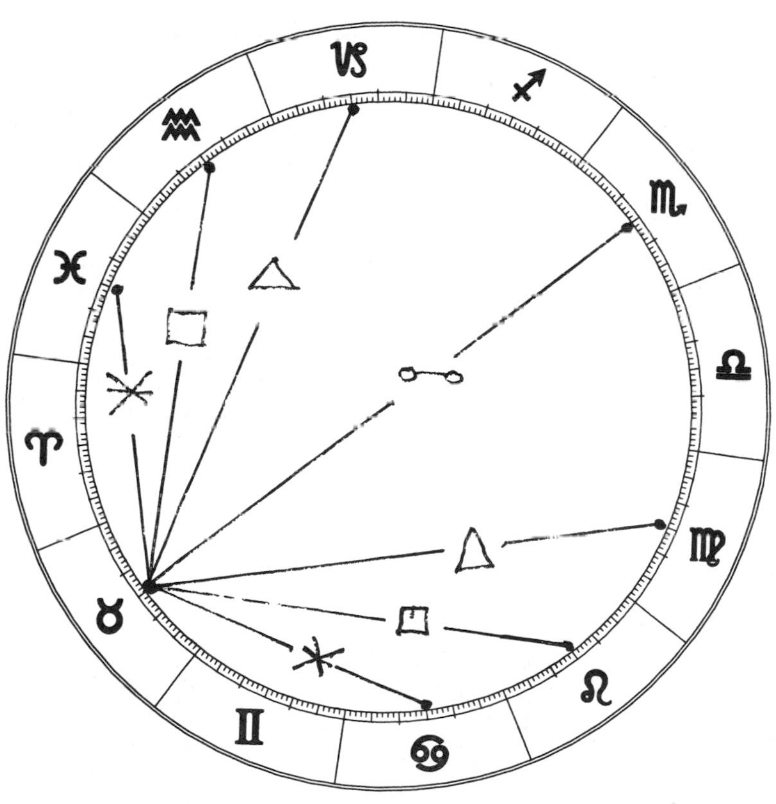

Appendix Five

EPHEMERIS

1943	♂	♃	♄	♅	♆	♇
Jan 1	11♐29	21♋34	6♊46	1♊11	2♎04	6♌40
15	21 29	19 42	6 03	0 49	2 02	6 22
Feb 1	3♑47	17 33	5 37	0 36	1 51	5 59
15	14 02	16 11	5 39	0 36	1 35	5 40
Mar 1	24 24	15 22	6 04	0 46	1 16	5 24
15	4♒50	15 11	6 49	1 06	0 54	5 10
Apr 1	17 36	15 48	8 08	1 43	0 26	4 59
15	28 10	16 57	9 29	2 21	0 04	4 55
May 1	10♓14	18 51	11 16	3 10	29♍42	4 58
15	20 45	20 58	12 58	3 58	29 28	5 05
Jun 1	3♈25	23 57	15 08	4 57	29 18	5 20
15	13 40	26 41	16 57	5 46	29 17	5 37
Jul 1	25 08	0♌01	19 00	6 38	29 23	6 01
15	4♉50	3 03	20 42	7 19	29 35	6 24
Aug 1	16 05	6 48	22 36	8 01	29 57	6 53
15	24 46	9 54	23 58	8 27	0♎21	7 17
Sep 1	4♊22	13 33	25 18	8 46	0 54	7 45
15	11 13	16 26	26 04	8 51	1 24	8 05
Oct 1	17 28	19 28	26 34	8 44	2 00	8 24
15	21 01	21 51	26 36	8 28	2 30	8 36
Nov 1	22 08	24 15	26 11	7 58	3 05	8 44
15	19 56	25 45	25 28	7 27	3 30	8 45
Dec 1	14 36	26 47	24 21	6 47	3 53	8 39
15	9♊25	27♌04	23♊14	6♊12	4♎06	8♌29

1944	♂	♃	♄	♅	♆	♇
Jan 1	5♊25	26♌32	21♊51	5♊34	4♎14	8♌12
15	5 00	25 26	20 53	5 10	4 14	7 54
Feb 1	7 36	23 30	20 02	4 53	4 04	7 31
15	11 40	21 40	19 43	4 50	3 49	7 12
Mar 1	17 20	19 47	19 46	4 58	3 29	6 53
15	23 31	18 20	20 12	5 16	3 07	6 40
Apr 1	1♋48	17 16	21 10	5 49	2 39	6 28
15	9 06	17 02	22 17	6 26	2 17	6 24
May 1	17 48	17 32	23 51	7 15	1 55	6 26
15	25 39	18 33	25 26	8 01	1 40	6 33
Jun 1	5♌27	20 27	27 31	9 01	1 30	6 49
15	13 41	22 28	29 18	9 50	1 28	7 06
Jul 1	23 15	25 10	1♋23	10 43	1 33	7 29
15	1♍46	27 48	3 10	11 26	1 45	7 52
Aug 1	12 16	1♍14	5 14	12 10	2 06	8 21
15	21 04	4 12	6 47	12 38	2 29	8 46
Sep 1	1♎55	7 52	8 24	13 00	3 02	9 14
15	11 01	10 54	9 28	13 08	3 32	9 34
Oct 1	21 36	14 17	10 20	13 04	4 08	9 54
15	1♏01	17 07	10 44	12 51	4 38	10 06
Nov 1	12 40	20 18	10 43	12 23	5 13	10 15
15	22 26	22 37	10 19	11 52	5 39	10 16
Dec 1	3♐48	24 49	9 28	11 13	6 02	10 11
15	13♐56	26♍16	8♋27	10♊37	6♎16	10♌01

1945	♂	♃	♄	♅	♆	♇
Jan 1	26♐25	27♍18	7♋04	9♊58	6♎25	9♌43
15	6♑52	27 29	5 57	9 32	6 25	9 26
Feb 1	19 44	26 52	4 49	9 12	6 16	9 02
15	0♒27	25 44	4 10	9 06	6 02	8 43
Mar 1	11 15	24 10	3 51	9 11	5 44	8 26
15	22 06	22 23	3 54	9 25	5 22	8 11
Apr 1	5♓19	20 16	4 27	9 56	4 54	7 59
15	16 12	18 51	5 17	10 30	4 32	7 55
May 1	28 34	17 49	6 34	11 17	4 09	7 56
15	9♈19	17 32	7 56	12 03	3 54	8 03
Jun 1	22 10	17 58	9 51	13 02	3 42	8 17
15	2♉35	18 57	11 34	13 52	3 39	8 34
Jul 1	14 15	20 39	13 37	14 46	3 43	8 57
15	24 11	22 35	15 26	15 31	3 54	9 20
Aug 1	5♊53	25 23	17 36	16 17	4 14	9 49
15	15 08	27 59	19 17	16 48	4 36	10 14
Sep 1	25 52	1♎23	21 09	17 14	5 08	10 43
15	4♋09	4 19	22 29	17 25	5 38	11 04
Oct 1	12 54	7 46	23 41	17 26	6 13	11 24
15	19 44	10 47	24 26	17 15	6 44	11 37
Nov 1	26 39	14 23	24 52	16 50	7 20	11 46
15	0♌46	17 12	24 50	16 21	7 46	11 48
Dec 1	3 08	20 11	24 21	15 43	8 10	11 44
15	2♌32	22♎30	23♋35	15♊07	8♎26	11♌35

1946	♂	♃	♄	♅	♆	♇
Jan 1	28♋17	24♎49	22♋21	14♊27	8♎36	11♌18
15	22 53	26 13	21 12	13 58	8 37	11 00
Feb 1	16 56	27 12	19 52	13 35	8 29	10 37
15	14 24	27 21	18 57	13 25	8 16	10 17
Mar 1	14 25	26 53	18 18	13 27	7 59	10 00
15	16 36	25 51	17 59	13 38	7 37	9 45
Apr 1	21 25	24 00	18 04	14 05	7 10	9 32
15	26 41	22 14	18 33	14 37	6 47	9 27
May 1	3♌42	20 16	19 29	15 22	6 24	9 27
15	10 29	18 50	20 37	16 07	6 08	9 33
Jun 1	19 19	17 44	22 17	17 05	5 55	9 47
15	26 59	17 27	23 52	17 55	5 50	10 03
Jul 1	6♍06	17 51	25 49	18 51	5 53	10 26
15	14 22	18 47	27 36	19 36	6 03	10 49
Aug 1	24 41	20 34	29 48	20 26	6 22	11 19
15	3♎26	22 30	1♌34	20 59	6 43	11 44
Sep 1	14 19	25 19	3 36	21 29	7 15	12 13
15	23 31	27 55	5 08	21 44	7 44	12 34
Oct 1	4♏17	1♏09	6 38	21 48	8 19	12 55
15	13 54	4 07	7 40	21 40	8 50	13 09
Nov 1	25 53	7 49	8 32	21 19	9 26	13 20
15	5♐57	10 53	8 52	20 52	9 53	13 22
Dec 1	17 41	14 18	8 47	20 15	10 18	13 19
15	28♐09	17♏10	8♌21	19♊39	10♎34	13♌10

1947	♂	♃	♄	♅	♆	♇
Jan 1	11♑04	20♏22	7♌23	18♊57	10♎46	12♌53
15	21 51	22 41	6 21	18 27	10 48	12 36
Feb 1	5♒05	25 00	4 58	18 00	10 42	12 12
15	16 04	26 25	3 53	17 47	10 30	11 53
Mar 1	27 05	27 17	2 57	17 45	10 13	11 35
15	8♓07	27 34	2 18	17 53	9 53	11 19
Apr 1	21 27	27 05	1 57	18 17	9 25	11 06
15	2♈22	26 04	2 04	18 46	9 02	11 00
May 1	14 42	24 22	2 37	19 29	8 38	11 00
15	25 22	22 37	3 26	20 12	8 21	11 05
Jun 1	8♉06	20 31	4 48	21 10	8 07	11 18
15	18 23	19 06	6 11	22 00	8 02	11 34
Jul 1	29 54	18 02	7 58	22 56	8 04	11 57
15	9♊45	17 42	9 40	23 43	8 12	12 20
Aug 1	21 24	18 05	11 50	24 35	8 30	12 49
15	0♋44	19 01	13 37	25 11	8 50	13 15
Sep 1	11 42	20 50	15 46	25 45	9 21	13 44
15	20 25	22 49	17 25	26 02	9 50	14 06
Oct 1	29 56	25 30	19 08	26 10	10 25	14 28
15	7♌51	28 09	20 26	26 07	10 56	14 43
Nov 1	16 45	1♐39	21 39	25 49	11 32	14 54
15	23 22	4 42	22 19	25 24	12 00	14 57
Dec 1	29 49	8 16	22 40	24 48	12 26	14 54
15	4♍12	11♐24	22♌34	24♊13	12♎43	14♌46

1948	♂	♃	♄	♅	♆	♇
Jan 1	7♍15	15♐08	21♌59	23♊30	12♎56	14♌30
15	7 20	18 04	21 10	22 58	13 00	14 13
Feb 1	4 01	21 21	19 54	22 28	12 55	13 50
15	29♌00	23 44	18 46	22 12	12 44	13 30
Mar 1	23 15	25 54	17 37	22 07	12 26	13 10
15	19 27	27 27	16 43	22 12	12 06	12 54
Apr 1	18 08	28 37	15 59	22 33	11 38	12 41
15	19 39	28 56	15 46	23 00	11 16	12 34
May 1	23 35	28 34	15 56	23 40	10 52	12 34
15	28 28	27 37	16 26	24 23	10 34	12 39
Jun 1	5♍42	25 51	17 29	25 20	10 19	12 52
15	12 27	24 06	18 38	26 09	10 13	13 08
Jul 1	20 52	22 07	20 13	27 06	10 14	13 30
15	28 43	20 38	21 47	27 54	10 22	13 53
Aug 1	8♎45	19 27	23 50	28 48	10 39	14 23
15	17 24	19 06	25 36	29 26	10 59	14 49
Sep 1	28 18	19 30	27 46	0♋02	11 29	15 18
15	7♏36	20 28	29 30	0 23	11 58	15 41
Oct 1	18 33	22 12	1♍22	0 34	12 33	16 03
15	28 24	24 13	2 50	0 33	13 04	16 18
Nov 1	10♐41	27 10	4 20	0 18	13 40	16 30
15	21 02	29 55	5 16	29♊56	14 08	16 34
Dec 1	3♑06	3♑19	5 58	29 21	14 35	16 31
15	13♑51	6♑27	6♍12	28♊47	14♎53	16♌23

EPHEMERIS

The abbreviated Ephemeris below lists the positions for Mars, Jupiter, Saturn, Uranus, Neptune and Pluto. These positions are listed for the 1st and the 15th of each month. For dates between those listed, simply estimate each Planet's position according to the distance traveled during the dates shown.

1949	♂	♃	♄	♅	♆	♇
Jan 1	27♑04	10♑22	6♍00	28♊03	15♎06	16♌08
15	8♒04	13 37	5 27	27 30	15 11	15 51
Feb 1	21 30	17 28	4 24	26 57	15 06	15 27
15	2♓34	20 29	3 20	26 39	14 56	15 07
Mar 1	13 37	23 19	2 13	26 31	14 40	14 48
15	24 36	25 53	1 09	26 33	14 21	14 32
Apr 1	7♈49	28 32	0 06	26 50	13 53	14 18
15	18 34	0♒14	29♌33	27 14	13 30	14 11
May 1	0♉40	1 34	29 19	27 52	13 06	14 09
15	11 05	2 07	29 29	28 32	12 48	14 14
Jun 1	23 30	1 58	0♍07	29 28	12 32	14 26
15	3♊32	1 11	1 00	0♋17	12 25	14 41
Jul 1	14 46	29♑39	2 18	1 15	12 25	15 04
15	24 24	27 57	3 41	2 04	12 31	15 26
Aug 1	5♋52	25 47	5 35	2 59	12 47	15 57
15	15 06	24 12	7 16	3 40	13 06	16 22
Sep 1	26 04	22 51	9 24	4 19	13 35	16 53
15	4♌53	22 22	11 09	4 43	14 03	17 16
Oct 1	14 42	22 35	13 07	4 58	14 38	17 38
15	23 03	23 26	14 43	5 01	15 09	17 54
Nov 1	2♍48	25 14	16 27	4 50	15 46	18 07
15	10 27	27 14	17 38	4 30	16 14	18 12
Dec 1	18 40	0♒02	18 40	3 58	16 42	18 10
15	25♍15	2♒49	19♍14	3♋25	17♎01	18♌03

1950	♂	♃	♄	♅	♆	♇
Jan 1	2♎13	6♒30	19♍26	2♋41	17♎16	17♌48
15	6 46	9 43	19 13	2 06	17 21	17 31
Feb 1	10 18	13 45	18 30	1 31	17 18	17 08
15	11 00	17 05	17 36	1 10	17 09	16 47
Mar 1	9 14	20 23	16 33	0 58	16 54	16 28
15	5 09	23 34	15 26	0 57	16 35	16 12
Apr 1	28♍40	27 12	14 11	1 09	16 08	15 56
15	24 16	29 56	13 22	1 31	15 45	15 48
May 1	22 03	2♓40	12 45	2 06	15 20	15 46
15	22 46	4 38	12 35	2 44	15 02	15 50
Jun 1	26 26	6 23	12 49	3 38	14 45	16 02
15	1♎11	7 13	13 23	4 27	14 37	16 17
Jul 1	8 02	7 26	14 23	5 24	14 35	16 39
15	14 57	6 56	15 32	6 14	14 40	17 01
Aug 1	24 18	5 34	17 13	7 12	14 55	17 31
15	2♏36	3 57	18 46	7 54	15 13	17 57
Sep 1	13 19	1 44	20 48	8 37	15 41	18 28
15	22 35	0 01	22 33	9 04	16 09	18 52
Oct 1	3♐37	28♒29	24 32	9 23	16 43	19 16
15	13 35	27 44	26 13	9 29	17 15	19 32
Nov 1	26 03	27 41	28 07	9 23	17 52	19 46
15	6♑35	28 23	29 30	9 06	18 20	19 51
Dec 1	18 50	29 54	0♎48	8 37	18 49	19 50
15	29♑42	1♓48	1♎39	8♋04	19♎09	19♌44

1951	♂	♃	♄	♅	♆	♇
Jan 1	13♒02	4♓42	2♎15	7♋21	19♎25	19♌29
15	24 03	7 27	2 21	6 46	19 31	19 13
Feb 1	7♓26	11 09	2 01	6 08	19 30	18 50
15	18 24	14 24	1 22	5 44	19 22	18 29
Mar 1	29 17	17 44	0 [illegible]	[illegible]	19 08	18 10
15	10♈04	21 08	29♍25	5 24	18 49	17 53
Apr 1	22 58	25 13	28 06	5 32	18 23	17 36
15	3♉25	28 30	27 06	5 50	18 00	17 28
May 1	15 10	2♈04	26 12	6 22	17 35	17 25
15	25 16	4 58	25 43	6 59	17 15	17 28
Jun 1	7♊18	8 07	25 33	7 51	16 57	17 39
15	17 02	10 20	25 47	8 39	16 48	17 54
Jul 1	27 59	12 19	26 [illegible]	9 38	16 45	18 15
15	7♋24	13 31	27 20	10 27	16 49	18 38
Aug 1	18 39	14 10	28 45	11 25	17 03	19 08
15	27 46	13 59	0♎08	12 10	17 20	19 34
Sep 1	8♌41	12 56	2 02	12 56	17 48	20 05
15	17 33	11 29	3 42	13 26	18 15	20 29
Oct 1	27 31	9 26	5 40	13 49	18 49	20 54
15	6♍07	7 35	7 23	13 59	19 20	21 11
Nov 1	16 22	5 40	9 24	13 56	19 57	21 28
15	24 38	4 39	10 55	13 43	20 26	21 32
Dec 1	3♎51	4 15	12 27	13 17	20 56	21 32
15	11♎38	4♈38	13♎32	12♋46	21♎16	21♌26

1952	♂	♃	♄	♅	♆	♇
Jan 1	20♎40	5♈57	14♎29	12♋03	21♎34	21♌13
15	27 37	7 40	14 54	11 27	21 41	20 57
Feb 1	5♏16	10 22	14 56	10 47	21 42	20 33
15	10 41	13 01	14 35	10 [illegible]	21 [illegible]	20 [illegible]
Mar 1	[illegible]	16 10	13 52	10 02	21 20	19 52
15	17 50	19 19	12 57	9 54	21 02	19 34
Apr 1	18 12	23 18	11 40	9 59	20 36	19 18
15	15 50	26 40	10 35	10 15	20 13	19 09
May 1	10 39	0♉31	9 30	10 44	19 48	19 06
15	5 40	3 49	8 46	11 18	19 28	19 08
Jun 1	1 44	7 40	8 16	12 09	19 09	19 19
15	1 14	10 [illegible]	8 13	12 56	19 00	19 33
Jul 1	3 52	13 45	8 32	13 53	18 56	19 55
15	8 12	16 08	9 10	14 44	18 59	20 17
Aug 1	15 28	18 30	10 18	15 44	19 12	20 48
15	22 40	19 55	11 30	16 30	19 29	21 14
Sep 1	2♐33	20 52	13 13	17 18	19 56	21 45
15	11 24	20 57	14 47	17 51	20 22	22 10
Oct 1	22 09	20 15	16 42	18 17	20 56	22 35
15	2♑00	19 00	18 24	18 30	21 27	22 53
Nov 1	14 23	16 55	20 27	18 31	22 05	23 08
15	24 50	15 01	22 04	18 20	22 34	23 15
Dec 1	7♒00	13 02	23 45	17 56	23 04	23 16
15	17♒45	11♉45	25♎01	17♋27	23♎25	23♌10

1953	♂	♃	♄	♅	♆	♇
Jan 1	0♓51	11♉01	26♎14	16♋45	23♎43	22♌57
15	11 38	11 08	26 54	16 09	23 52	22 41
Feb 1	24 39	12 11	27 17	15 28	23 52	22 18
15	5♈16	13 41	27 13	14 59	23 46	21 57
Mar 1	15 46	15 40	26 48	14 39	23 33	21 37
15	26 07	18 04	26 07	14 28	23 16	21 19
Apr 1	8♉31	21 24	24 58	14 28	22 51	21 02
15	18 33	24 23	23 55	14 40	22 28	20 52
May 1	29 49	28 00	22 43	15 06	22 02	20 48
15	9♊32	1♊15	21 47	15 38	21 42	20 50
Jun 1	21 09	5 14	20 58	16 26	21 22	21 00
15	0♋34	8 30	20 37	17 12	21 12	21 14
Jul 1	11 11	12 06	20 36	18 08	21 07	21 35
15	20 23	15 07	20 55	18 59	21 09	21 57
Aug 1	1♌25	18 29	21 44	20 00	21 20	22 27
15	10 26	20 57	22 42	20 48	21 36	22 54
Sep 1	21 17	23 27	24 11	21 39	22 02	23 26
15	0♍10	25 01	25 37	22 14	22 28	23 51
Oct 1	10 15	26 09	27 25	22 44	23 01	24 16
15	19 02	26 29	29 05	23 01	23 32	24 35
Nov 1	29 38	26 00	1♏08	23 06	24 10	24 51
15	8♎18	24 55	2 48	22 59	24 40	24 59
Dec 1	18 09	23 06	4 36	22 39	25 10	25 01
15	26♎41	21♊13	6♏01	22♋12	25♎[illegible]	24♌56

1954	♂	♃	♄	♅	♆	♇
Jan 1	6♏55	19♊01	7♏29	21♋32	25♎52	24♌43
15	15 13	17 34	8 24	20 55	26 01	24 28
Feb 1	25 02	16 34	9 07	20 13	26 03	24 05
15	2♐53	16 27	9 21	19 42	25 58	23 45
Mar 1	10 24	16 59	9 14	19 19	25 47	23 24
15	17 30	18 07	8 48	19 04	25 30	23 06
Apr 1	25 20	20 12	7 53	19 00	25 05	22 48
15	0♑50	22 22	6 56	19 09	24 42	22 37
May 1	5 40	25 16	5 43	19 31	24 16	22 32
15	8 06	28 04	4 42	20 00	23 56	22 34
Jun 1	8 05	1♋42	3 38	20 46	23 35	22 43
15	5 27	4 49	3 01	21 30	23 24	22 56
Jul 1	0 42	8 26	2 40	22 25	23 17	23 16
15	27♐03	11 36	2 42	23 16	23 19	23 38
Aug 1	25 38	15 22	3 10	24 18	23 29	24 09
15	27 25	18 20	3 53	25 07	23 43	24 35
Sep 1	2♑39	21 41	5 06	26 01	24 08	25 08
15	8 51	24 09	6 21	26 39	24 34	25 33
Oct 1	17 26	26 34	8 00	27 12	25 07	26 00
15	25 52	28 13	9 35	27 32	25 37	26 19
Nov 1	6♒54	29 31	11 36	27 42	26 15	26 37
15	16 26	29 56	13 17	27 39	26 45	26 45
Dec 1	27 39	29 37	15 09	27 22	27 16	26 48
15	7♓07	28♋41	16♏41	26♋58	27♎39	26♌44

EPHEMERIS

The abbreviated Ephemeris below lists the positions for Mars, Jupiter, Saturn, Uranus, Neptune and Pluto. These positions are listed for the 1st and the 15th of each month. For dates between those listed, simply estimate each Planet's position according to the distance traveled during the dates shown.

1955	♂	♃	♄	♅	♆	♇
Jan 1	19♓49	26♋51	18♏20	26♋20	28♎00	26♌32
15	29 52	25 01	19 28	25 44	28 11	26 17
Feb 1	12♈01	22 48	20 30	25 00	28 14	25 55
15	21 57	21 18	21 00	24 28	28 10	25 34
Mar 1	1♉48	20 17	21 11	24 02	28 00	25 13
15	11 32	19 53	21 01	23 44	27 44	24 54
Apr 1	23 14	20 15	20 24	23 36	27 19	24 36
15	2♊44	21 12	19 37	23 41	26 57	24 25
May 1	13 28	22 55	18 30	23 59	26 31	24 18
15	22 45	24 53	17 27	24 25	26 10	24 19
Jun 1	3♋54	27 45	16 14	25 07	25 48	24 27
15	13 00	0♌23	15 25	25 50	25 36	24 40
Jul 1	23 20	3 39	14 46	26 44	25 29	25 00
15	2♌19	6 38	14 31	27 35	25 29	25 22
Aug 1	13 10	10 22	14 38	28 37	25 37	25 52
15	22 05	13 27	15 04	29 27	25 51	26 19
Sep 1	2♍55	17 08	16 00	0♌23	26 15	26 51
15	11 49	20 02	17 03	1 04	26 40	27 17
Oct 1	22 02	23 09	18 31	1 41	27 12	27 45
15	0♎59	25 37	19 59	2 04	27 43	28 05
Nov 1	11 53	28 09	21 55	2 19	28 21	28 23
15	20 54	29 47	23 34	2 19	28 51	28 33
Dec 1	1♏15	1♍02	25 28	2 06	29 23	28 37
15	10♏21	1♍29	27♏05	1♌45	29♎47	28♌34

1956	♂	♃	♄	♅	♆	♇
Jan 1	21♏26	1♍12	28♏53	1♌09	0♏09	28♌23
15	0♐35	0 17	0♐12	0 34	0 20	28 08
Feb 1	11 44	28♌29	1 29	29♋50	0 25	27 46
15	20 55	26 42	2 14	29 16	0 22	27 25
Mar 1	0♑46	24 45	2 42	28 45	0 12	27 03
15	9 56	23 12	2 48	28 25	29♎56	26 44
Apr 1	20 59	21 55	2 29	28 14	29 32	26 24
15	0♒01	21 30	1 54	28 15	29 10	26 13
May 1	10 08	21 46	0 56	28 30	28 44	26 06
15	18 44	22 37	29♏56	28 54	28 23	26 07
Jun 1	28 42	24 20	28 41	29 34	28 01	26 14
15	6♓16	26 13	27 44	0♌15	27 48	26 27
Jul 1	13 51	28 48	26 51	1 08	27 40	26 47
15	19 07	1♍21	26 22	1 58	27 39	27 08
Aug 1	23 01	4 42	26 10	3 01	27 47	27 39
15	23 32	7 38	26 21	3 52	28 00	28 05
Sep 1	20 48	11 17	27 00	4 49	28 23	28 39
15	17 02	14 19	27 50	5 32	28 48	29 05
Oct 1	13 45	17 44	29 06	6 12	29 20	29 33
15	13 17	20 37	0♐26	6 38	29 50	29 54
Nov 1	16 04	23 52	2 15	6 56	0♏28	0♍13
15	20 33	26 16	3 51	6 59	0 59	0 23
Dec 1	27 22	28 36	5 45	6 50	1 31	0 27
15	4♈21	0♎11	7♐24	6♌31	1♏55	0♍25

1957	♂	♃	♄	♅	♆	♇
Jan 1	13♈41	1♎26	9♐18	5♌57	2♏18	0♍14
15	21 50	1 48	10 44	5 23	2 30	0 00
Feb 1	2♉04	1 25	12 13	4 39	2 36	29♌38
15	10 42	0 26	13 11	4 04	2 33	29 17
Mar 1	19 24	28♍59	13 52	3 33	2 25	28 56
15	28 11	27 14	14 14	3 10	2 10	28 36
Apr 1	8♊52	25 05	14 15	2 54	1 47	28 16
15	17 40	23 33	13 55	2 52	1 25	28 04
May 1	27 43	22 20	13 11	3 03	0 59	27 57
15	6♋30	21 52	12 18	3 24	0 37	27 56
Jun 1	17 09	22 05	11 05	4 00	0 15	28 03
15	25 55	22 54	10 03	4 39	0 01	28 15
Jul 1	5♌57	24 27	9 00	5 30	29♎51	28 34
15	14 44	26 15	8 18	6 20	29 50	28 55
Aug 1	25 26	28 56	7 47	7 22	29 56	29 25
15	4♍17	1♎27	7 41	8 13	0♏08	29 52
Sep 1	15 06	4 47	8 00	9 13	0 30	0♍26
15	24 04	7 42	8 36	9 57	0 54	0 53
Oct 1	4♎25	11 08	9 38	10 41	1 25	1 21
15	13 33	14 10	10 47	11 10	1 56	1 43
Nov 1	24 46	17 47	12 26	11 33	2 34	2 03
15	4♏06	20 39	13 58	11 40	3 04	2 14
Dec 1	14 54	23 43	15 49	11 35	3 37	2 20
15	24♏27	26♎07	17♐28	11♌19	4♏02	2♍18

1958	♂	♃	♄	♅	♆	♇
Jan 1	6♐12	28♎35	19♐26	10♌49	4♏26	2♍08
15	15 59	0♏08	20 58	10 16	4 39	1 55
Feb 1	28 01	1 20	22 39	9 32	4 46	1 33
15	8♑02	1 40	23 48	8 56	4 45	1 12
Mar 1	18 08	1 23	24 43	8 24	4 37	0 51
15	28 19	0 31	25 21	7 58	4 24	0 31
Apr 1	10♒47	28♎49	25 42	7 37	4 01	0 10
15	21 05	27 05	25 37	7 32	3 40	29♌57
May 1	2♓52	25 04	25 10	7 39	3 14	29 49
15	13 09	23 32	24 28	7 55	2 52	29 47
Jun 1	25 30	22 15	23 22	8 29	2 28	29 53
15	5♈30	21 47	22 21	9 05	2 14	0♍04
Jul 1	16 37	21 58	21 12	9 54	2 03	0 23
15	25 57	22 44	20 19	10 42	2 00	0 44
Aug 1	6♉36	24 21	19 31	11 44	2 05	1 14
15	14 35	26 11	19 10	12 36	2 16	1 41
Sep 1	22 55	28 53	19 09	13 37	2 38	2 14
15	28 14	1♏25	19 29	14 24	3 00	2 42
Oct 1	1♊54	4 35	20 14	15 10	3 31	3 11
15	2 23	7 32	21 11	15 42	4 01	3 33
Nov 1	29♉10	11 14	22 39	16 09	4 39	3 55
15	24 19	14 18	24 04	16 20	5 10	4 07
Dec 1	19 06	17 46	25 50	16 20	5 43	4 13
15	16♉46	20♏41	27♐28	16♌08	6♏09	4♍13

1959	♂	♃	♄	♅	♆	♇
Jan 1	17♉26	23♏58	29♐28	15♌40	6♏34	4♍04
15	20 24	26 24	1♑05	15 10	6 48	3 51
Feb 1	26 05	28 53	2 53	14 27	6 57	3 30
15	1♊57	0♐27	4 13	13 50	6 57	3 09
Mar 1	8 33	1 29	5 20	13 16	6 50	2 48
15	15 39	1 58	6 12	12 47	6 37	2 27
Apr 1	24 47	1 43	6 52	12 23	6 16	2 06
15	2♋35	0 52	7 04	12 14	5 55	1 52
May 1	11 44	29♏19	6 54	12 16	5 29	1 43
15	19 53	27 37	6 26	12 30	5 06	1 40
Jun 1	29 56	25 29	5 31	12 59	4 42	1 45
15	8♌20	23 56	4 35	13 32	4 27	1 55
Jul 1	18 02	22 41	3 25	14 19	4 15	2 14
15	26 38	22 10	2 25	15 06	4 11	2 34
Aug 1	7♍11	22 20	1 24	16 08	4 15	3 04
15	15 59	23 06	0 49	17 00	4 25	3 31
Sep 1	26 49	24 45	0 28	18 02	4 45	4 05
15	5♎52	26 36	0 32	18 50	5 07	4 33
Oct 1	16 22	29 11	1 00	19 39	5 37	5 03
15	25 41	1♐46	1 44	20 14	6 06	5 26
Nov 1	7♏12	5 13	2 58	20 46	6 44	5 48
15	16 51	8 14	4 14	21 00	7 15	6 01
Dec 1	28 03	11 48	5 53	21 04	7 49	6 09
15	8♐01	14♐58	7♑28	20♌56	[illegible]♏15	6♍09

1960	♂	♃	♄	♅	♆	♇
Jan 1	20♐18	18♐44	9♑27	20♌32	8♏41	6♍02
15	0♑35	21 44	11 06	20 04	8 57	5 49
Feb 1	13 15	25 07	13 01	19 22	9 07	5 29
15	23 48	27 37	14 29	18 45	9 08	5 08
Mar 1	5♒12	29 55	15 51	18 08	9 02	4 45
15	15 56	1♑38	16 55	17 37	8 50	4 25
Apr 1	29 01	3 03	17 51	17 10	8 29	4 02
15	9♓49	3 34	18 18	16 58	8 08	3 48
May 1	22 07	3 26	18 25	16 57	7 42	3 38
15	2♈49	2 40	18 11	17 07	7 19	3 35
Jun 1	15 39	1 04	17 31	17 33	6 55	3 40
15	26 03	29♐23	16 42	18 05	6 39	3 50
Jul 1	7♉42	27 22	15 35	18 49	6 27	4 07
15	17 36	25 46	14 34	19 35	6 22	4 28
Aug 1	29 13	24 22	13 24	20 36	6 25	4 57
15	8♊21	23 50	12 37	21 28	6 34	5 25
Sep 1	18 48	23 59	12 00	22 30	6 53	5 59
15	26 44	24 46	11 49	23 20	7 15	6 27
Oct 1	4♋51	26 20	12 00	24 11	7 45	6 58
15	10 50	28 13	12 30	24 48	8 14	7 21
Nov 1	16 11	1♑02	13 30	25 23	8 52	7 44
15	18 26	3 43	14 37	25 41	9 23	7 58
Dec 1	17 54	7 04	16 08	25 48	9 57	8 07
15	14♋33	10♑11	17♑38	25♌43	10♏24	8♍08

EPHEMERIS

The abbreviated Ephemeris below lists the positions for Mars, Jupiter, Saturn, Uranus, Neptune and Pluto. These positions are listed for the 1st and the 15th of each month. For dates between those listed, simply estimate each Planet's position according to the distance traveled during the dates shown.

1961	♂	♃	♄	♅	♆	♇
Jan 1	8♋07	14♑05	19♑35	25♌23	10♏50	8♍00
15	3 13	17 21	21 14	24 56	11 06	7 49
Feb 1	0 10	21 15	23 13	24 16	11 17	7 28
15	0 28	24 21	24 47	23 39	11 19	7 08
Mar 1	2 55	27 16	26 12	23 03	11 14	6 46
15	6 58	29 56	27 27	22 31	11 03	6 25
Apr 1	13 26	2♒46	28 40	22 00	10 43	6 02
15	19 38	4 38	29 22	21 45	10 22	5 47
May 1	27 25	6 12	29 48	21 39	9 56	5 36
15	4♌41	6 58	29 50	21 46	9 34	5 32
Jun 1	13 57	7 06	29 20	22 08	9 09	5 36
15	21 52	6 31	28 50	22 36	8 52	5 45
Jul 1	1♍11	5 11	27 52	23 18	8 39	6 02
15	9 33	3 34	26 52	24 02	8 33	6 22
Aug 1	19 57	1 23	25 38	25 01	8 35	6 51
15	28 43	29♑42	24 42	25 53	8 43	7 18
Sep 1	9♎36	28 08	23 49	26 56	9 01	7 53
15	18 45	27 26	23 22	27 47	9 21	8 21
Oct 1	29 26	27 24	23 15	28 40	9 50	8 52
15	8♏59	28 03	23 29	29 20	10 19	9 17
Nov 1	20 49	29 38	24 11	29 59	10 57	9 41
15	0♐47	1♒29	25 06	0♍20	11 28	9 56
Dec 1	12 23	4 09	26 26	0 32	12 03	10 06
15	22♐43	6♒50	27♑49	0♍31	12♏30	10♍08

1962	♂	♃	♄	♅	♆	♇
Jan 1	5♑28	10♒28	29♑41	0♍15	12♏57	10♍02
15	16 09	13 39	1♒19	29♌51	13 14	9 51
Feb 1	29 15	17 39	3 20	29 13	13 27	9 31
15	10♒09	21 00	4 58	28 37	13 29	9 11
Mar 1	21 06	24 20	6 30	28 00	13 26	8 49
15	2♓06	27 04	7 55	27 26	13 16	8 28
Apr 1	15 25	1♓18	9 22	26 52	12 56	8 04
15	26 21	4 08	10 18	26 34	12 36	7 48
May 1	8♈44	7 02	11 03	26 24	12 11	7 36
15	19 26	9 10	11 22	26 27	11 48	7 32
Jun 1	2♉15	11 09	11 19	26 44	11 23	7 34
15	12 36	12 12	10 56	27 09	11 05	7 42
Jul 1	24 12	12 41	10 11	27 48	10 51	7 58
15	4♊06	12 26	9 17	28 30	10 44	8 18
Aug 1	15 48	11 19	8 03	29 27	10 44	8 47
15	25 08	9 50	7 02	0♍18	10 51	9 14
Sep 1	6♋03	7 40	5 56	1 22	11 08	9 48
15	14 39	5 52	5 15	2 14	11 28	10 17
Oct 1	23 59	4 08	4 49	3 09	11 56	10 49
15	1♌35	3 10	4 47	3 51	12 24	11 14
Nov 1	9 56	2 50	5 11	4 34	13 02	11 40
15	15 50	3 17	5 51	4 59	13 33	11 56
Dec 1	21 08	4 34	6 58	5 15	14 08	12 07
15	24♌01	6♓17	8♒11	5♍18	14♏36	12♍10

1963	♂	♃	♄	♅	♆	♇
Jan 1	24♌35	9♓00	9♒56	5♍06	15♏04	12♍05
15	22 12	11 40	11 31	4 46	15 22	11 55
Feb 1	16 21	15 16	13 32	4 10	15 36	11 35
15	10 55	18 27	15 12	3 35	15 40	11 16
Mar 1	6 55	21 46	16 50	[illegible]	[illegible]	10 [illegible]
15	[illegible] 21	[illegible] 09	18 22	2 23	15 28	10 32
Apr 1	6 40	29 15	20 02	1 47	15 10	10 08
15	9 52	2♈34	21 11	1 25	14 51	9 52
May 1	15 11	6 12	22 13	1 11	14 25	9 39
15	20 55	9 12	22 48	1 10	14 03	9 33
Jun 1	28 52	12 29	23 06	1 22	13 37	9 34
15	6♍02	14 50	23 00	1 44	13 18	9 41
Jul 1	14 45	17 02	22 31	2 20	13 03	9 57
15	22 46	18 26	21 48	2 59	12 55	10 16
Aug 1	2♎56	19 22	20 40	3 55	12 54	10 44
15	11 36	19 26	19 38	4 45	13 00	11 11
Sep 1	22 30	18 40	18 24	5 49	13 15	11 46
15	1♏45	17 23	17 31	6 41	13 34	12 15
Oct 1	12 37	15 26	16 48	7 38	14 02	12 48
15	22 22	13 34	16 29	8 23	14 30	13 14
Nov 1	4♐31	11 30	16 32	9 00	15 07	13 40
15	14 45	10 15	16 57	9 37	15 38	13 57
Dec 1	26 42	9 34	17 48	9 58	16 13	14 09
15	7♑20	9♈42	18♒51	10♍04	16♏42	14♍14

1964	♂	♃	♄	♅	♆	♇
Jan 1	20♑26	10♈44	20♒25	9♍57	17♏11	14♍10
15	1♒22	12 15	21 54	9 40	17 30	14 01
Feb 1	14 44	14 46	23 52	9 08	17 45	13 42
15	26 40	17 [illegible]	[illegible]	[illegible] 01	17 50	13 23
Mar 1	7♓39	20 19	27 21	7 55	17 48	13 00
15	18 41	23 23	28 59	7 19	17 40	12 38
Apr 1	1♈58	27 19	0♓49	6 40	17 22	12 13
15	12 48	0♉39	2 09	6 16	17 03	11 56
May 1	25 01	4 29	3 25	5 59	16 38	11 43
15	5♉32	7 49	4 15	5 55	16 15	11 36
Jun 1	18 05	11 43	4 52	6 04	15 49	11 37
15	28 13	14 46	5 02	6 23	15 30	11 44
Jul 1	9♊34	17 58	4 50	6 56	15 14	11 59
15	19 17	20 28	4 20	7 33	15 06	12 17
Aug 1	0♋50	23 01	3 23	8 27	15 04	12 46
15	10 06	24 36	2 24	9 16	15 09	13 13
Sep 1	21 05	25 49	1 08	10 19	15 24	13 48
15	29 52	26 08	0 07	11 12	15 42	14 17
Oct 1	9♌35	25 41	29♒11	12 10	16 09	14 50
15	17 47	24 38	20 37	12 57	16 37	15 17
Nov 1	27 15	22 42	28 21	13 45	17 14	15 44
15	4♍34	20 50	28 30	14 16	17 45	16 02
Dec 1	12 13	18 45	29 04	14 40	18 20	16 15
15	18♍06	17♉17	29♒55	14♍50	18♏49	16♍20

1965	♂	♃	♄	♅	♆	♇
Jan 1	23♍49	16♉15	1♓17	14♍47	19♏19	16♍17
15	26 54	16 08	2 40	14 33	19 39	16 08
Feb 1	27 59	16 54	4 33	14 03	19 54	15 50
15	26 10	18 11	6 12	13 31	20 00	15 31
Mar 1	22 00	20 00	7 55	12 55	19 59	15 09
15	16 35	22 15	9 36	12 18	19 52	14 47
Apr 1	11 01	25 26	11 35	11 38	19 35	14 22
15	8 52	28 21	13 04	11 11	19 17	14 04
May 1	9 27	1♊53	14 34	10 50	18 52	13 49
15	12 11	5 05	15 39	10 42	18 29	13 42
Jun 1	17 37	9 03	16 37	10 46	18 03	13 42
15	23 22	12 19	17 05	11 02	17 44	13 48
Jul 1	0♎59	15 57	17 13	11 31	17 27	14 02
15	8 22	19 00	16 59	12 05	17 17	14 20
Aug 1	18 04	22 27	16 19	12 56	17 14	14 48
15	26 33	25 01	15 29	13 44	17 18	15 14
Sep 1	7♏23	27 40	14 15	14 47	17 32	15 49
15	16 41	29 24	13 11	15 40	17 49	16 19
Oct 1	27 42	0♋44	12 03	16 39	18 15	16 53
15	7♐38	1 17	11 15	17 27	18 42	17 20
Nov 1	20 03	1 04	10 38	18 19	19 19	17 49
15	0♑31	0 11	10 29	18 53	19 50	18 07
Dec 1	12 44	28♊31	10 44	19 21	20 26	18 22
15	23♑34	26♊42	11♓19	19♍35	20♏55	18♍28

1966	♂	♃	♄	♅	♆	♇
Jan 1	6♒53	24♊26	12♓26	19♍37	21♏26	18♍26
15	17 55	22 51	13 38	19 26	21 46	18 18
Feb 1	1♓21	21 35	15 22	19 00	22 03	18 01
15	12 23	21 15	16 58	18 30	22 10	17 42
Mar 1	23 21	21 34	18 39	17 55	22 10	17 21
15	4♈14	22 30	20 23	17 19	22 04	16 59
Apr 1	17 17	24 21	22 27	16 37	21 49	16 33
15	27 52	26 23	24 04	16 07	21 31	16 15
May 1	9♉46	29 08	25 46	15 43	21 07	15 59
15	20 00	1♋50	27 04	15 31	20 44	15 51
Jun 1	2♊11	5 23	28 21	15 31	20 17	15 49
15	12 03	8 28	29 06	15 42	19 57	15 54
Jul 1	23 06	12 03	29 36	16 07	19 39	16 07
15	2♋37	15 13	29 41	16 39	19 29	16 24
Aug 1	13 57	19 00	29 20	17 27	19 24	16 52
15	23 07	22 00	28 44	18 14	19 27	17 18
Sep 1	4♌03	25 25	27 40	19 15	19 40	17 53
15	12 54	27 58	26 38	20 08	19 56	18 23
Oct 1	22 50	0♌30	25 24	21 08	20 21	18 57
15	1♍20	2 18	24 25	21 58	20 48	19 25
Nov 1	11 25	3 48	23 29	22 52	21 24	19 55
15	19 29	4 25	23 02	23 29	21 55	20 15
Dec 1	28 22	4 20	22 56	24 01	22 31	20 30
15	5♎46	3♌35	23♓13	24♍19	23♏00	20♍38

EPHEMERIS

The abbreviated Ephemeris below lists the positions for Mars, Jupiter, Saturn, Uranus, Neptune and Pluto. These positions are listed for the 1st and the 15th of each month. For dates between those listed, simply estimate each Planet's position according to the distance traveled during the dates shown.

1967	♂	♃	♄	♅	♆	♇
Jan 1	14♎07	1♌55	24♓01	24♍25	23♏32	20♍38
15	20 19	0 09	25 00	24 19	23 53	20 31
Feb 1	26 41	27♋54	26 32	23 57	24 12	20 15
15	0♏35	26 17	28 02	23 29	24 20	19 56
Mar 1	2 50	25 06	29 39	22 56	24 21	19 35
15	2 57	24 29	1♈22	22 20	24 16	19 13
Apr 1	29♎47	24 36	3 29	21 36	24 02	18 47
15	25 00	25 22	5 12	21 05	23 45	18 28
May 1	19 12	26 54	7 03	20 37	23 21	18 11
15	15 51	28 44	8 32	20 22	22 58	18 02
Jun 1	15 11	1♌27	10 06	20 17	22 31	17 58
15	17 18	4 00	11 08	20 25	22 11	18 02
Jul 1	22 02	7 11	11 58	20 46	21 52	18 15
15	27 43	10 08	12 22	21 14	21 41	18 31
Aug 1	6♏03	13 49	12 25	21 59	21 35	18 58
15	13 50	16 54	12 06	22 44	21 37	19 24
Sep 1	24 10	20 35	11 18	23 44	21 48	19 59
15	3♐15	23 32	10 23	24 36	22 03	20 29
Oct 1	14 10	26 43	9 10	25 37	22 28	21 04
15	24 07	29 15	8 05	26 28	22 53	21 33
Nov 1	6♑35	1♍55	6 54	27 24	23 29	22 03
15	17 07	3 41	6 10	28 04	24 00	22 24
Dec 1	29 21	5 07	5 43	28 40	24 36	22 41
15	10♒12	5♍45	5♈40	29♍01	25♏06	22♍50

1968	♂	♃	♄	♅	♆	♇
Jan 1	23♒26	5♍41	6♈06	29♍13	25♏38	22♍51
15	4♓22	4 57	6 50	29 10	26 01	22 45
Feb 1	17 34	3 20	8 07	28 52	26 20	22 30
15	28 22	1 36	9 27	28 27	26 29	22 12
Mar 1	9♈48	29♌38	11 04	27 54	26 32	21 50
15	20 21	27 59	12 44	27 18	26 27	21 28
Apr 1	2♉57	26 30	14 51	26 34	26 14	21 01
15	13 10	25 54	16 36	26 01	25 57	20 42
May 1	24 38	25 57	18 35	25 31	25 34	20 24
15	4♊30	26 38	20 12	25 13	25 11	20 14
Jun 1	16 16	28 09	21 59	25 05	24 44	20 10
15	25 49	29 55	23 15	25 09	24 24	20 14
Jul 1	6♋33	2♍22	24 24	25 27	24 04	20 25
15	15 50	4 50	25 06	25 52	23 53	20 42
Aug 1	26 57	8 08	25 31	26 35	23 46	21 08
15	5♌59	11 01	25 30	27 18	23 47	21 34
Sep 1	16 52	14 39	25 01	28 16	23 57	22 09
15	25 44	17 41	24 18	29 08	24 12	22 40
Oct 1	5♍47	21 07	23 12	0♎09	24 36	23 15
15	14 29	24 02	22 07	1 01	25 01	23 44
Nov 1	24 58	27 21	20 48	1 59	25 36	24 15
15	3♎29	29 51	19 51	2 41	26 08	24 37
Dec 1	13 06	2♎18	19 05	3 20	26 44	24 55
15	21♎22	4♎01	18♈44	3♎44	27♏14	25♍04

1969	♂	♃	♄	♅	♆	♇
Jan 1	1♏11	5♎27	18♈48	3♎59	27♏47	25♍06
15	9 01	6 00	19 15	3 59	28 09	25 01
Feb 1	18 07	5 51	20 14	3 45	28 29	24 47
15	25 11	5 03	21 22	3 23	28 39	24 29
Mar 1	1♐40	3 43	22 44	2 53	28 43	24 09
15	7 24	2 03	24 17	2 19	28 39	23 46
Apr 1	12 56	29♍52	26 20	1 34	28 27	23 19
15	15 51	28 14	28 06	1 00	28 11	22 59
May 1	16 41	26 51	0♉08	0 27	27 48	22 41
15	14 51	26 13	1 52	0 06	27 26	22 30
Jun 1	9 53	26 13	3 51	29♍53	26 59	22 25
15	5 18	26 51	5 19	29 54	26 38	22 27
Jul 1	2 04	28 14	6 46	0♎07	26 18	22 37
15	2 01	29 55	7 46	0 29	26 05	22 53
Aug 1	5 21	2♎29	8 35	1 08	25 57	23 18
15	10 20	4 55	8 55	1 49	25 57	23 44
Sep 1	18 23	8 12	8 51	2 46	26 06	24 19
15	26 13	11 04	8 25	3 36	26 20	24 50
Oct 1	6♑08	14 29	7 34	4 37	26 43	25 25
15	15 26	17 31	6 35	5 29	27 07	25 55
Nov 1	27 18	21 11	5 14	6 30	27 42	26 27
15	7♒23	24 05	4 08	7 14	28 13	26 50
Dec 1	19 09	27 14	3 04	7 56	28 49	27 09
15	29♒33	29♎43	2♉25	8♎23	29♏19	27♍20

1970	♂	♃	♄	♅	♆	♇
Jan 1	12♓14	2♏20	2♉04	8♎43	29♏53	27♍24
15	22 40	4 01	2 10	8 47	0♐17	27 19
Feb 1	5♈15	5 25	2 47	8 38	0 38	27 06
15	15 30	5 56	3 39	8 19	0 49	26 50
Mar 1	25 39	5 50	4 48	7 52	0 53	26 29
15	5♉40	5 09	6 12	7 19	0 51	26 07
Apr 1	17 39	3 36	8 07	6 35	0 40	25 39
15	27 23	1 56	9 50	5 59	0 25	25 19
May 1	8♊21	29♎55	11 52	5 24	0 03	24 59
15	17 49	28 17	13 40	5 00	29♏41	24 48
Jun 1	29 09	26 49	15 47	4 43	29 14	24 41
15	8♋23	26 11	17 25	4 40	28 52	24 42
Jul 1	18 49	26 09	19 07	4 49	28 32	24 52
15	27 53	26 46	20 23	5 07	28 18	25 06
Aug 1	8♌49	28 12	21 35	5 42	28 09	25 31
15	17 46	29 54	22 15	6 20	28 08	25 56
Sep 1	28 36	2♏29	22 37	7 15	28 15	26 31
15	7♍30	4 57	22 32	8 04	28 28	27 01
Oct 1	17 39	8 04	22 01	9 04	28 50	27 37
15	26 32	10 58	21 14	9 57	29 14	28 07
Nov 1	7♎20	14 39	20 00	10 59	29 48	28 41
15	16 13	17 44	18 53	11 45	0♐18	29 05
Dec 1	26 23	21 14	17 38	12 30	0 54	29 25
15	5♏17	24♏12	16♉42	13♎01	1♐25	29♍37

1971	♂	♃	♄	♅	♆	♇
Jan 1	16♏04	27♏35	15♉57	13♎25	2♐00	29♍42
15	24 55	0♐06	15 42	13 34	2 24	29 40
Feb 1	5♐37	2 44	15 54	13 29	2 46	29 27
15	14 22	4 27	16 27	13 13	2 58	29 12
Mar 1	23 01	5 41	17 20	12 49	3 04	28 52
15	1♑34	6 21	18 30	12 17	3 03	28 30
Apr 1	11 41	6 21	20 13	11 34	2 53	28 02
15	19 45	5 41	21 50	10 58	2 39	27 41
May 1	28 30	4 16	23 49	10 21	2 18	27 20
15	5♒34	2 39	25 37	9 54	1 56	27 07
Jun 1	13 03	0 30	27 48	9 33	1 29	26 59
15	17 54	28♏52	29 33	9 26	1 07	27 00
Jul 1	21 18	27 27	1♊26	9 31	0 45	27 08
15	21 52	26 45	2 55	9 46	0 31	27 21
Aug 1	19 21	26 41	4 27	10 17	0 20	27 45
15	15 46	27 16	5 26	10 52	0 18	28 10
Sep 1	12 22	28 44	6 14	11 44	0 24	28 44
15	12 05	0♐27	6 31	12 32	0 36	29 15
Oct 1	14 51	2 55	6 24	13 31	0 57	29 51
15	19 31	5 26	5 56	14 24	1 20	0♎22
Nov 1	27 10	8 49	4 57	15 27	1 54	0 56
15	4♓36	11 48	3 55	16 15	2 24	1 21
Dec 1	13 55	15 22	2 37	17 03	3 00	1 43
15	22♓32	18♐32	1♊31	17♎37	3♐31	1♎56

1972	♂	♃	♄	♅	♆	♇
Jan 1	3♈23	22♐21	0♊25	18♎05	4♐06	2♎03
15	12 30	25 24	29♉50	18 17	4 31	2 01
Feb 1	23 40	28 53	29 35	18 17	4 55	1 51
15	2♉55	1♑29	29 47	18 05	5 08	1 36
Mar 1	12 49	3 56	0♊23	17 42	5 15	1 15
15	22 01	5 48	1 18	17 12	5 14	0 53
Apr 1	3♊08	7 26	2 46	16 30	5 05	0 25
15	12 14	8 10	4 14	15 54	4 52	0 03
May 1	22 35	8 16	6 06	15 16	4 31	29♍42
15	1♋34	7 42	7 51	14 47	4 09	29 29
Jun 1	12 26	6 18	10 03	14 23	3 42	29 20
15	21 20	4 42	11 51	14 13	3 20	29 19
Jul 1	1♌28	2 40	13 52	14 14	2 58	29 27
15	10 20	0 59	15 30	14 26	2 43	29 39
Aug 1	21 06	29♐24	17 18	14 54	2 32	0♎03
15	29 58	28 39	18 32	15 26	2 29	0 27
Sep 1	10♍47	28 33	19 42	16 16	2 34	1 01
15	19 44	29 09	20 19	17 03	2 46	1 32
Oct 1	0♎01	0♑32	20 36	18 01	3 05	2 09
15	9 05	2 16	20 27	18 54	3 28	2 40
Nov 1	20 10	4 57	19 50	19 57	4 01	3 15
15	29 23	7 33	18 59	20 46	4 32	3 40
Dec 1	10♏01	10 50	17 46	21 36	5 08	4 03
15	19♏24	13♑55	16♊37	22♎13	5♐39	4♎17

EPHEMERIS

The abbreviated Ephemeris below lists the positions for Mars, Jupiter, Saturn, Uranus, Neptune and Pluto. These positions are listed for the 1st and the 15th of each month. For dates between those listed, simply estimate each Planet's position according to the distance traveled during the dates shown.

1973	♂	♃	♄	♅	♆	♇
Jan 1	0♐54	17♑49	15♊18	22♎45	6♐14	4♎25
15	10 28	21 05	14 26	23 00	6 39	4 24
Feb 1	22 11	25 02	13 47	23 03	7 04	4 14
15	1♑55	28 11	13 38	22 54	7 18	4 00
Mar 1	11 44	1♒11	13 51	22 35	7 25	3 41
15	21 36	3 57	14 26	22 08	7 26	3 19
Apr 1	0♒00	6 56	15 34	21 28	7 18	2 51
15	13 35	8 58	16 48	20 52	7 05	2 29
May 1	24 56	10 45	18 29	20 12	6 45	2 07
15	4♓48	11 44	20 07	19 41	6 24	1 53
Jun 1	16 37	12 08	22 15	19 13	5 57	1 42
15	26 07	11 46	24 04	19 00	5 35	1 41
Jul 1	6♈32	10 39	26 08	18 57	5 12	1 47
15	15 07	9 10	27 54	19 05	4 56	1 58
Aug 1	24 30	7 01	29 54	19 28	4 44	2 21
15	1♉01	5 15	1♋22	19 58	4 40	2 44
Sep 1	6 47	3 30	2 52	20 44	4 44	3 18
15	9 05	2 35	3 49	21 29	4 54	3 49
Oct 1	8 22	2 18	4 31	22 26	5 13	4 25
15	4 56	2 44	4 45	23 19	5 35	4 57
Nov 1	29♈22	4 04	4 33	24 23	6 07	5 33
15	26 08	5 47	4 00	25 13	6 37	6 00
Dec 1	25 28	8 17	3 01	26 05	7 13	6 24
15	27♈32	10♒53	1♋56	26♎44	7♐44	6♎39

1974	♂	♃	♄	♅	♆	♇
Jan 1	2♉33	14♒25	0♋33	27♎20	8♐20	6♎49
15	8 08	17 33	29♊28	27 39	8 46	6 49
Feb 1	16 04	21 32	28 27	27 47	9 12	6 41
15	23 16	24 53	27 56	27 42	9 27	6 27
Mar 1	0♊52	28 14	27 47	27 26	9 35	6 09
15	8 45	1♓31	28 00	27 02	9 37	5 47
Apr 1	18 35	5 20	28 44	26 23	9 31	5 19
15	26 50	8 16	29 41	25 48	9 19	4 57
May 1	6♋22	11 17	1♋06	25 07	8 59	4 34
15	14 47	13 34	2 34	24 35	8 39	4 18
Jun 1	25 06	15 47	4 34	24 04	8 12	4 07
15	3♌39	17 03	6 19	23 47	7 49	4 04
Jul 1	13 29	17 48	8 24	23 40	7 26	4 08
15	22 09	17 47	10 12	23 44	7 10	4 19
Aug 1	2♍46	16 55	12 20	24 03	6 56	4 40
15	11 35	15 36	13 59	24 29	6 51	5 03
Sep 1	22 25	13 31	15 45	25 12	6 53	5 37
15	1♎26	11 41	16 59	25 55	7 02	6 07
Oct 1	11 51	9 48	18 03	26 51	7 20	6 44
15	21 06	8 38	18 39	27 42	7 41	7 16
Nov 1	2♏30	8 00	18 54	28 46	8 13	7 53
15	12 01	8 13	18 43	29 38	8 42	8 20
Dec 1	23 04	9 15	18 04	0♏32	9 18	8 46
15	2♐52	10♓47	17♋12	1♏13	9♐50	9♎02

1975	♂	♃	♄	♅	♆	♇
Jan 1	14♐58	13♓19	15♋52	1♏53	10♐26	9♎13
15	25 04	15 51	14 43	2 15	10 53	9 15
Feb 1	7♑29	19 20	13 27	2 28	11 19	9 08
15	17 51	22 28	12 37	2 26	11 36	8 58
Mar 1	28 19	25 45	12 07	2 14	11 45	8 38
15	8♒53	29 06	11 57	1 53	11 48	8 17
Apr 1	21 47	3♈13	12 14	1 17	11 43	7 49
15	2♓26	6 34	12 51	0 43	11 32	7 26
May 1	14 37	10 16	13 57	0 02	11 13	7 03
15	25 13	13 20	15 11	29♎28	10 53	6 46
Jun 1	7♈59	16 44	16 58	28 54	10 26	6 33
15	18 19	19 13	18 37	28 34	10 04	6 23
Jul 1	29 53	21 36	20 37	28 22	9 40	6 32
15	9♉43	23 11	22 25	28 23	9 23	6 42
Aug 1	21 10	24 23	24 37	28 38	9 08	7 02
15	0♊05	24 42	26 22	29 00	9 02	7 24
Sep 1	10 07	24 13	28 20	29 40	9 03	7 57
15	17 30	23 08	29 47	0♏21	9 11	8 27
Oct 1	24 40	21 20	1♌11	1 14	9 28	9 04
15	29 23	19 28	2 06	2 05	9 48	9 36
Nov 1	2♋27	17 17	2 48	3 09	10 19	10 14
15	2 09	15 51	2 59	4 01	10 48	10 42
Dec 1	28♊25	14 54	2 44	4 56	11 23	11 09
15	23♊12	14♈47	2♌09	5♏40	11♐55	11♎26

1976	♂	♃	♄	♅	♆	♇
Jan 1	17♊22	15♈32	1♌04	6♏23	12♐32	11♎40
15	14 57	16 51	29♋58	6 49	12 59	11 43
Feb 1	15 29	19 08	28 35	7 06	13 28	11 37
15	18 16	21 31	27 32	7 08	13 43	11 26
Mar 1	22 57	24 26	26 40	6 59	13 55	11 08
15	28 28	27 25	26 11	6 40	13 58	10 47
Apr 1	6♋10	1♉17	26 03	6 06	13 54	10 19
15	13 07	4 35	26 20	5 33	13 44	9 56
May 1	21 31	8 25	27 04	4 52	13 26	9 32
15	29 11	11 45	28 03	4 18	13 06	9 16
Jun 1	8♌48	15 41	29 34	3 42	12 39	9 01
15	16 55	18 47	1♌03	3 20	12 17	8 56
Jul 1	26 24	22 06	2 56	3 05	11 53	8 58
15	4♍52	24 42	4 41	3 02	11 35	9 07
Aug 1	15 20	27 25	6 52	3 13	11 20	9 26
15	24 07	29 11	8 39	3 33	11 13	9 48
Sep 1	4♎59	0♊38	10 45	4 10	11 13	10 20
15	14 06	1 10	12 21	4 48	11 20	10 51
Oct 1	24 43	1 00	13 59	5 40	11 36	11 27
15	4♏11	0 09	15 09	6 30	11 56	12 00
Nov 1	15 54	28♉24	16 13	7 33	12 26	12 38
15	25 44	26 35	16 43	8 26	12 55	13 07
Dec 1	7♐11	24 26	16 52	9 23	13 31	13 35
15	17♐23	22♉49	16♌36	10♏07	14♐02	13♎53

1977	♂	♃	♄	♅	♆	♇
Jan 1	29♐59	21♉32	15♌50	10♏53	14♐39	14♎07
15	10♑30	21 10	14 54	11 21	15 07	14 11
Feb 1	23 28	21 38	13 33	11 42	15 35	14 07
15	4♒15	22 43	12 25	11 47	15 52	13 56
Mar 1	15 07	24 21	11 24	11 42	16 04	13 40
15	26 01	26 27	10 37	11 26	16 09	13 20
Apr 1	9♓17	29 29	10 03	10 56	16 06	12 52
15	20 12	2♊18	9 58	10 24	15 57	12 29
May 1	2♈35	5 45	10 18	9 44	15 40	12 04
15	13 19	8 55	10 57	9 09	15 20	11 46
Jun 1	26 10	12 51	12 09	8 31	14 54	11 31
15	6♉35	16 06	13 24	8 06	14 31	11 25
Jul 1	18 13	19 46	15 05	7 47	14 07	11 25
15	28 09	22 51	16 43	7 41	13 48	11 33
Aug 1	9♊52	26 23	18 50	7 48	13 32	11 51
15	19 10	29 02	20 37	8 04	13 24	12 12
Sep 1	29 59	1♋50	22 47	8 37	13 23	12 44
15	8♋26	3 42	24 29	9 13	13 29	13 13
Oct 1	17 26	5 15	26 17	10 02	13 44	13 50
15	24 37	6 00	27 41	10 50	14 03	14 23
Nov 1	2♌09	6 03	29 04	11 53	14 32	15 02
15	7 04	5 22	29 54	12 46	15 00	15 32
Dec 1	10 41	3 53	0♍27	13 43	15 36	16 00
15	11♌22	2♋09	0♍32	14♏30	16♐07	16♎20

1978	♂	♃	♄	♅	♆	♇
Jan 1	9♌03	29♊52	0♍10	15♏19	16♐45	16♎36
15	4 24	28 10	29♌29	15 50	17 13	16 41
Feb 1	27♋47	26 41	28 20	16 15	17 42	16 39
15	23 48	26 07	27 14	16 24	18 00	16 29
Mar 1	22 17	26 12	26 07	16 22	18 13	16 14
15	23 12	26 56	25 06	16 10	18 19	15 54
Apr 1	26 54	28 34	24 11	15 43	18 17	15 27
15	1♌30	0♋26	23 45	15 13	18 09	15 03
May 1	7 59	3 03	23 41	14 34	17 53	14 38
15	14 26	5 39	23 59	13 59	17 34	14 19
Jun 1	22 59	9 07	24 48	13 19	17 08	14 03
15	0♍29	12 08	25 47	12 52	16 46	13 55
Jul 1	9 28	15 42	27 13	12 30	16 21	13 55
15	17 39	18 51	28 41	12 20	16 02	14 01
Aug 1	27 55	22 38	0♍39	12 22	15 44	14 18
15	6♎38	25 40	2 23	12 35	15 35	14 38
Sep 1	17 32	29 09	4 32	13 03	15 33	15 08
15	26 45	1♌47	6 17	13 36	15 38	15 38
Oct 1	7♏32	4 26	8 13	14 23	15 51	16 14
15	17 13	6 22	9 46	15 10	16 09	16 48
Nov 1	29 15	8 04	11 25	16 12	16 38	17 27
15	9♐22	8 52	12 31	17 04	17 06	17 57
Dec 1	21 11	9 01	13 25	18 03	17 41	18 27
15	1♑43	8♌27	13♍51	18♏51	18♐12	18♎48

EPHEMERIS

The abbreviated Ephemeris below lists the positions for Mars, Jupiter, Saturn, Uranus, Neptune and Pluto. These positions are listed for the 1st and the 15th of each month. For dates between those listed, simply estimate each Planet's position according to the distance traveled during the dates shown.

1979	♂	♃	♄	♅	♆	♇
Jan 1	14♑42	7♌00	13♍54	19♏42	18♐50	19♎06
15	25 33	5 19	13 32	20 16	19 19	19 13
Feb 1	8♒51	3 04	12 40	20 45	19 49	19 12
15	19 52	1 20	11 42	20 58	20 08	19 03
Mar 1	0♓54	0 00	10 36	21 00	20 22	18 49
15	11 57	29♋12	9 30	20 51	20 29	18 30
Apr 1	25 17	29 04	8 19	20 28	20 29	18 03
15	6♈11	29 38	7 36	20 00	20 21	17 39
May 1	18 29	0♌58	7 08	19 22	20 06	17 14
15	29 07	2 39	7 06	18 47	19 49	16 54
Jun 1	11♉47	5 13	7 31	18 06	19 23	16 36
15	22 02	7 40	8 12	17 37	19 00	16 28
Jul 1	3♊30	10 46	9 20	17 11	18 35	16 26
15	13 19	13 40	10 35	16 59	18 16	16 31
Aug 1	24 56	17 19	12 21	16 56	17 57	16 46
15	4♋15	20 23	13 58	17 05	17 47	17 05
Sep 1	15 15	24 06	16 03	17 30	17 43	17 35
15	24 00	27 04	17 49	18 00	17 47	18 04
Oct 1	3♌37	0♍18	19 47	18 44	18 00	18 40
15	11 40	2 55	21 27	19 29	18 17	19 13
Nov 1	20 49	5 43	23 18	20 29	18 44	19 53
15	27 45	7 36	24 36	21 21	19 11	20 24
Dec 1	4♍44	9 12	25 48	22 20	19 46	20 55
15	9♍46	10♍02	26♍33	23♏09	20♐17	21♎18

1980	♂	♃	♄	♅	♆	♇
Jan 1	13♍58	10♍12	26♍59	24♏03	20♐55	21♎37
15	15 20	9 39	26 58	24 39	21 25	21 45
Feb 1	13 44	8 12	26 28	25 12	21 55	21 46
15	9 42	6 33	25 43	25 29	22 16	21 39
Mar 1	3 54	4 36	24 40	25 34	22 31	21 24
15	29♌04	2 52	23 35	25 28	22 39	21 06
Apr 1	26 03	1 14	22 16	25 08	22 40	20 39
15	26 19	0 26	21 21	24 43	22 33	20 15
May 1	29 11	0 16	20 35	24 06	22 19	19 49
15	3♍24	0 46	20 14	23 32	22 01	19 29
Jun 1	10 05	2 06	20 16	22 50	21 36	19 11
15	16 31	3 43	20 40	22 19	21 13	19 01
Jul 1	24 41	6 03	21 29	21 52	20 48	18 58
15	2♎23	8 25	22 30	21 36	20 28	19 03
Aug 1	12 19	11 38	24 03	21 30	20 09	19 17
15	20 55	14 28	25 32	21 36	19 59	19 35
Sep 1	1♏48	18 05	27 30	21 57	19 54	20 04
15	11 06	21 06	29 12	22 25	19 57	20 33
Oct 1	22 04	24 33	1♎11	23 06	20 09	21 09
15	1♐57	27 30	2 54	23 50	20 25	21 42
Nov 1	14 16	0♎53	4 51	24 49	20 52	22 23
15	24 40	3 27	6 19	25 40	21 19	22 54
Dec 1	6♑47	6 02	7 45	26 40	21 54	23 26
15	17♑34	7♎53	8♎43	27♏30	22♐25	23♎49

1981	♂	♃	♄	♅	♆	♇
Jan 1	0♒50	9♎30	9♎30	28♏25	23♐03	24♎09
15	11 51	10 14	9 46	29 03	23 33	24 18
Feb 1	25 18	10 18	9 38	29 39	24 04	24 20
15	6♓22	9 41	9 08	29 58	24 25	24 14
Mar 1	17 24	8 30	8 21	0♐06	24 40	24 02
15	28 21	6 55	7 23	0 04	24 49	23 44
Apr 1	11♈31	4 45	6 04	29♏48	24 51	23 18
15	22 13	3 03	5 01	29 25	24 46	22 54
May 1	4♉16	1 30	4 00	28 51	24 33	22 28
15	14 37	0 41	3 22	28 17	24 16	22 07
Jun 1	26 58	0 28	3 01	27 35	23 51	21 47
15	6♊57	0 56	3 05	27 02	23 28	21 37
Jul 1	18 07	2 08	3 33	26 32	23 03	21 32
15	27 43	3 41	4 18	26 14	22 43	21 35
Aug 1	9♋08	6 07	5 34	26 03	22 22	21 48
15	18 21	8 28	6 51	26 06	22 11	22 05
Sep 1	29 19	11 40	8 39	26 23	22 05	22 33
15	8♌09	14 30	10 16	26 47	22 07	23 01
Oct 1	18 01	17 54	12 12	27 25	22 18	23 37
15	26 25	20 56	13 55	28 07	22 33	24 10
Nov 1	6♍18	24 36	15 57	29 04	22 59	24 51
15	14 07	27 33	17 32	29 54	23 25	25 23
Dec 1	22 37	0♏46	19 09	0♐54	23 59	25 56
15	29♍31	3♏20	20♎21	1♐44	24♐31	26♎20

1982	♂	♃	♄	♅	♆	♇
Jan 1	7♎03	6♏04	21♎27	2♐41	25♐09	26♎42
15	12 17	7 54	22 01	3 22	25 39	26 52
Feb 1	16 59	9 30	22 15	4 01	26 11	26 56
15	18 59	10 12	22 03	4 23	26 33	26 51
Mar 1	18 45	10 18	21 32	4 35	26 49	26 40
15	16 03	9 47	20 45	4 37	26 59	26 23
Apr 1	10 09	8 25	19 32	4 25	27 03	25 57
15	4 59	6 51	18 28	4 05	26 58	25 34
May 1	1 08	4 49	17 18	3 33	26 46	25 07
15	0 27	3 08	16 27	3 00	26 30	24 46
Jun 1	2 46	1 30	15 45	2 18	26 06	24 25
15	6 44	0 41	15 30	1 45	25 44	24 13
Jul 1	12 58	0 27	15 38	1 12	25 18	24 07
15	19 32	0 53	16 05	0 51	24 57	24 09
Aug 1	28 35	2 08	17 01	0 36	24 36	24 20
15	6♏45	3 41	18 05	0 35	24 24	24 36
Sep 1	17 21	6 08	19 40	0 48	24 17	25 03
15	26 34	8 31	21 10	1 09	24 18	25 30
Oct 1	7♐34	11 34	23 01	1 44	24 27	26 05
15	17 33	14 26	24 42	2 23	24 41	26 39
Nov 1	0♑02	18 06	26 45	3 18	25 06	27 19
15	10 34	21 11	28 24	4 07	25 32	27 52
Dec 1	22 49	24 42	0♏10	5 06	26 05	28 26
15	3♒41	27♏43	1♏32	5♐58	26♐36	28♎51

1983	♂	♃	♄	♅	♆	♇
Jan 1	17♒00	1♐11	2♏54	6♐56	27♐15	29♎14
15	28 00	3 47	3 44	7 39	27 45	29 26
Feb 1	11♓20	6 34	4 19	8 21	28 18	29 32
15	22 15	8 25	4 26	8 46	28 41	29 28
Mar 1	3♈04	9 48	4 12	9 02	28 58	29 18
15	13 46	10 40	3 39	9 07	29 09	29 03
Apr 1	26 35	10 54	2 39	8 59	29 14	28 38
15	6♉58	10 25	1 38	8 42	29 11	28 15
May 1	18 37	9 12	0 26	8 12	29 00	27 48
15	28 39	7 40	29♎26	7 41	28 45	27 26
Jun 1	10♊36	5 33	28 28	6 59	28 21	27 04
15	20 17	3 50	27 57	6 25	27 59	26 51
Jul 1	1♋09	2 16	27 43	5 51	27 33	26 43
15	10 32	1 23	27 52	5 27	27 12	26 44
Aug 1	21 44	1 05	28 29	5 09	26 50	26 53
15	0♌50	1 30	29 18	5 04	26 37	27 08
Sep 1	11 45	2 45	0♏38	5 12	26 29	27 33
15	20 37	4 20	1 58	5 30	26 28	28 00
Oct 1	0♍37	6 40	3 40	6 01	26 36	28 35
15	9 16	9 06	5 17	6 38	26 50	29 08
Nov 1	19 36	12 24	7 20	7 30	27 13	29 49
15	27 58	15 21	9 00	8 19	27 38	0♏22
Dec 1	7♎20	18 54	10 51	9 17	28 11	0 56
15	15♎19	22♐04	12♏21	10♐09	28♐42	1♏23

1984	♂	♃	♄	♅	♆	♇
Jan 1	24♎40	25♐55	13♏56	11♐08	29♐21	1♏47
15	1♏59	29 00	15 00	11 53	29 51	2 01
Feb 1	10 14	2♑34	15 54	12 38	0♑25	2 08
15	16 19	5 16	16 18	13 06	0 48	2 06
Mar 1	21 52	7 50	16 22	13 26	1 08	1 56
15	25 46	9 51	16 04	13 34	1 20	1 41
Apr 1	28 13	11 42	15 18	13 29	1 25	1 17
15	27 47	12 37	14 26	13 14	1 23	0 54
May 1	24 20	12 58	13 16	12 47	1 13	0 27
15	19 32	12 36	12 13	12 17	0 58	0 05
Jun 1	14 05	11 24	11 04	11 36	0 35	29♎42
15	11 51	9 54	10 20	11 02	0 13	29 29
Jul 1	12 32	7 54	9 49	10 26	29♐47	29 20
15	15 39	6 10	9 42	10 00	29 26	29 19
Aug 1	21 53	4 24	9 59	9 39	29 03	29 28
15	28 32	3 29	10 34	9 32	28 50	29 42
Sep 1	7♐56	3 08	11 38	9 37	28 41	0♏07
15	16 33	3 32	12 47	9 52	28 40	0 33
Oct 1	27 05	4 42	14 21	10 20	28 47	1 07
15	6♑48	6 18	15 52	10 54	28 59	1 40
Nov 1	19 04	8 50	17 51	11 45	29 23	2 21
15	29 26	11 20	19 31	12 32	29 47	2 54
Dec 1	11♒30	14 33	21 24	13 30	0♑20	3 29
15	22♒09	17♑35	22♏59	14♐22	0♑51	3♏56

EPHEMERIS

The abbreviated Ephemeris below lists the positions for Mars, Jupiter, Saturn, Uranus, Neptune and Pluto. These positions are listed for the 1st and the 15th of each month. For dates between those listed, simply estimate each Planet's position according to the distance traveled during the dates shown.

1985	♂	♃	♄	♅	♆	♇
Jan 1	5♓08	21♑27	24♏44	15♐22	1♑29	4♏22
15	15 49	24 44	25 58	16 07	2 00	4 36
Feb 1	28 42	28 42	27 08	16 55	2 34	4 44
15	9♈12	1♒54	27 46	17 25	2 58	4 43
Mar 1	19 36	4 58	28 05	17 46	3 17	4 36
15	29 51	7 50	28 05	17 57	3 30	4 22
Apr 1	12♉06	10 57	27 38	17 57	3 37	3 58
15	22 02	13 08	26 57	17 46	3 35	3 36
May 1	3♊12	15 06	25 55	17 22	3 26	3 09
15	12 50	16 17	24 53	16 54	3 13	2 46
Jun 1	24 21	16 56	23 38	16 14	2 50	2 22
15	3♋42	16 48	22 44	15 39	2 29	2 08
Jul 1	14 16	15 54	21 57	15 02	2 03	1 58
15	23 24	14 34	21 34	14 34	1 41	1 56
Aug 1	4♌24	12 29	21 30	14 10	1 18	2 02
15	13 24	10 41	21 48	13 59	1 03	2 15
Sep 1	24 15	8 46	22 34	14 00	0 53	2 38
15	3♍08	7 40	23 30	14 11	0 51	3 03
Oct 1	13 15	7 08	24 51	14 36	0 57	3 37
15	22 04	7 21	26 15	15 07	1 08	4 09
Nov 1	2♎44	8 27	28 07	15 55	1 30	4 51
15	11 30	9 59	29 45	16 41	1 54	5 24
Dec 1	21 27	12 20	1♐39	17 38	2 26	6 00
15	0♏08	14♒49	3♐17	18♐29	2♑57	6♏28

1986	♂	♃	♄	♅	♆	♇
Jan 1	10♏34	18♒15	5♐10	19♐30	3♑35	6♏56
15	19 05	21 20	6 33	20 17	4 06	7 11
Feb 1	29 15	25 18	7 57	21 07	4 41	7 21
15	7♐27	28 38	8 50	21 40	5 06	7 21
Mar 1	15 26	2♓00	9 25	22 04	5 25	7 14
15	23 08	5 19	9 41	22 18	5 39	7 02
Apr 1	1♑56	9 12	9 34	22 22	5 48	6 40
15	8 32	12 13	9 08	22 14	5 48	6 17
May 1	15 05	15 21	8 18	21 53	5 40	5 51
15	19 33	17 46	7 22	21 27	5 27	5 27
Jun 1	22 43	20 11	6 07	20 49	5 05	5 03
15	22 53	21 38	5 07	20 14	4 44	4 47
Jul 1	20 13	22 38	4 07	19 36	4 18	4 36
15	16 17	22 51	3 29	19 07	3 56	4 32
Aug 1	12 18	22 16	3 06	18 39	3 33	4 37
15	11 28	21 07	3 07	18 26	3 17	4 48
Sep 1	14 00	19 10	3 34	18 22	3 05	5 10
15	18 34	17 19	4 15	18 30	3 02	5 36
Oct 1	25 46	15 20	5 23	18 51	3 07	6 07
15	3♒20	13 58	6 36	19 19	3 17	6 39
Nov 1	13 34	13 04	8 20	20 04	3 38	7 20
15	22 36	13 03	9 54	20 48	4 01	7 54
Dec 1	3♓19	13 50	11 46	21 44	4 32	8 31
15	12♓56	15♓10	13♐26	22♐34	5♑03	8♏59

1987	♂	♃	♄	♅	♆	♇
Jan 1	24♓45	17♓31	15♐23	23♐36	5♑41	9♏28
15	4♈32	19 55	16 53	24 24	6 13	9 45
Feb 1	16 24	23 17	18 29	25 16	6 48	9 56
15	26 07	26 21	19 35	25 51	7 13	9 58
Mar 1	6♉16	29 36	20 25	26 18	7 34	9 53
15	15 21	2♈55	20 57	26 36	7 49	9 42
Apr 1	26 51	7 02	21 10	26 44	7 59	9 20
15	6♊13	10 24	20 59	26 39	8 00	8 59
May 1	16 49	14 09	20 25	26 22	7 53	8 32
15	26 00	17 16	19 38	25 58	7 41	8 09
Jun 1	7♋04	20 48	18 29	25 21	7 20	7 43
15	16 06	23 24	17 27	24 48	7 00	7 27
Jul 1	26 21	25 56	16 19	24 09	6 34	7 14
15	5♌18	27 42	15 30	23 38	6 12	7 09
Aug 1	16 07	29 09	14 48	23 07	5 47	7 12
15	25 01	29 41	14 33	22 51	5 31	7 22
Sep 1	5♍50	29 29	14 40	22 43	5 18	7 43
15	14 46	28 37	15 06	22 48	5 14	8 06
Oct 1	24 59	26 58	15 58	23 05	5 17	8 38
15	3♎59	25 10	17 00	23 30	5 26	9 09
Nov 1	14 57	22 54	18 33	24 12	5 46	9 50
15	24 02	21 19	20 01	24 54	6 08	10 24
Dec 1	4♏29	20 08	21 49	25 48	6 39	11 01
15	13♏41	19♈46	23♐28	26♐38	7♑09	11♏30

1988	♂	♃	♄	♅	♆	♇
Jan 1	24♏55	20♈14	25♐28	27♐40	7♑47	12♏00
15	4♐14	21 20	27 03	28 29	8 19	12 10
Feb 1	15 36	23 25	28 49	29 22	8 56	12 [illegible]
15	26 00	25 09	0♑05	0♑00	9 21	12 36
Mar 1	5♑06	28 27	1 12	0 32	9 43	12 31
15	14 33	1♉21	1 57	0 52	9 59	12 20
Apr 1	26 01	5 08	2 28	1 02	10 10	12 00
15	5♒26	8 24	2 32	1 00	10 11	11 39
May 1	16 06	12 13	2 14	0 46	10 06	11 12
15	25 17	15 33	1 39	0 24	9 54	10 49
Jun 1	6♓07	19 31	0 39	29♐49	9 34	10 28
15	14 37	22 40	29♐39	29 16	9 13	10 06
Jul 1	23 36	26 03	28 29	28 37	8 48	9 52
15	0♈32	28 46	27 32	28 05	8 25	9 46
Aug 1	7 10	1♊37	26 36	27 33	8 01	9 48
15	10 32	3 33	26 07	27 14	7 44	9 57
Sep 1	11 16	5 13	25 56	27 03	7 30	10 17
15	8 55	5 59	26 08	27 05	7 25	10 39
Oct 1	4 24	6 04	26 44	27 19	7 28	11 10
15	1 02	5 26	27 34	27 42	7 36	11 41
Nov 1	29♓58	3 53	28 55	28 22	7 55	12 22
15	1♈52	2 09	0♑16	29 02	8 17	12 56
Dec 1	6 30	29♉59	1 59	29 54	8 47	13 33
15	12♈05	28♉15	3♑35	0♑44	9♑17	14♏03

1989	♂	♃	♄	♅	♆	♇
Jan 1	20♈12	26♉44	5♑36	1♑45	9♑55	14♏34
15	27 36	26 08	7 14	2 35	10 27	14 53
Feb 1	7♉10	26 20	9 06	3 30	11 03	15 07
15	15 21	27 12	10 31	4 09	11 29	15 11
Mar 1	23 43	28 38	11 43	4 40	11 52	15 08
15	2♊13	0♊35	12 42	5 03	12 08	14 59
Apr 1	12 37	3 28	13 32	5 18	12 20	14 40
15	21 14	6 11	13 53	5 19	12 23	14 19
May 1	1♋07	9 33	13 53	5 08	12 18	13 53
15	9 47	12 40	13 32	4 49	12 08	13 30
Jun 1	20 19	16 34	12 46	4 17	11 49	13 03
15	29 01	19 49	11 53	3 45	11 29	12 45
Jul 1	8♌58	23 29	10 44	3 06	11 03	12 30
15	17 43	26 36	9 43	2 33	10 41	12 23
Aug 1	28 23	0♋12	8 36	1 58	10 15	12 23
15	7♍13	2 56	7 53	1 37	9 58	12 31
Sep 1	18 02	5 52	7 23	1 22	9 43	12 49
15	27 02	7 53	7 19	1 21	9 37	13 10
Oct 1	7♎24	9 37	7 37	1 31	9 38	13 41
15	16 34	10 33	8 13	1 51	9 46	14 11
Nov 1	27 50	10 52	9 19	2 27	10 04	14 51
15	7♏15	10 24	10 30	3 05	10 24	15 25
Dec 1	18 08	9 07	12 05	3 56	10 54	16 03
15	27♏46	7♋29	13♑27	4♑44	11♑20	16♏33

1990	♂	♃	♄	♅	♆	♇
Jan 1	9♐39	5♋13	15♑36	5♑45	12♑01	17♏05
15	19 33	3 26	17 15	6 35	12 33	17 25
Feb 1	1♑44	1 44	19 13	7 32	13 09	17 41
15	11 53	0 58	20 45	8 13	13 37	17 47
Mar 1	22 08	0 50	22 07	8 47	13 59	17 46
15	2♒28	1 21	23 18	9 12	14 17	17 37
Apr 1	15 07	2 46	24 25	9 31	14 31	17 20
15	25 34	4 29	25 01	9 35	14 34	17 00
May 1	7♓32	6 57	25 20	9 28	14 31	16 34
15	17 58	9 27	25 15	9 12	14 22	16 11
Jun 1	0♈31	12 49	24 46	8 42	14 03	15 44
15	10 41	15 47	24 04	8 11	13 44	15 24
Jul 1	22 01	19 18	23 01	7 33	13 19	15 08
15	1♉36	22 26	22 00	6 59	12 56	15 00
Aug 1	12 39	26 14	20 46	6 23	12 30	14 59
15	21 06	29 18	19 53	5 59	12 12	15 05
Sep 1	0♊15	2♌50	19 06	5 41	11 56	15 21
15	6 35	5 32	18 46	5 36	11 49	15 41
Oct 1	11 54	8 18	18 45	5 43	11 49	16 11
15	14 19	10 21	19 06	5 59	11 55	16 40
Nov 1	13 38	12 15	19 55	6 32	12 12	17 20
15	10 03	13 13	20 55	7 07	12 32	17 54
Dec 1	4 11	13 36	22 19	7 56	13 00	18 32
15	29♉50	13♌14	23♑45	8♑43	13♑29	19♏03

EPHEMERIS

The abbreviated Ephemeris below lists the positions for Mars, Jupiter, Saturn, Uranus, Neptune and Pluto. These positions are listed for the 1st and the 15th of each month. For dates between those listed, simply estimate each Planet's position according to the distance traveled during the dates shown.

1991	♂	♃	♄	♅	♆	♇
Jan 1	27♉45	11♌59	25♑40	9♑44	14♑07	19♏36
15	28 51	10 25	27 19	10 34	14 39	19 57
Feb 1	2♊54	8 11	29 20	11 31	15 16	20 15
15	7 48	6 24	0♒56	12 14	15 44	20 22
Mar 1	13 41	4 55	2 26	12 50	16 07	20 22
15	20 16	3 56	3 47	13 19	16 26	20 15
Apr 1	28 56	3 33	5 09	13 41	16 41	19 58
15	6♋26	3 55	6 00	13 49	16 46	19 40
May 1	15 20	5 03	6 38	13 45	16 44	19 14
15	23 19	6 35	6 50	13 32	16 35	18 51
Jun 1	3♌13	9 00	6 40	13 05	16 18	18 24
15	11 31	11 21	6 11	12 35	15 59	18 04
Jul 1	21 08	14 22	5 20	11 58	15 34	17 46
15	29 41	17 12	4 23	11 24	15 12	17 37
Aug 1	10♍12	20 49	3 08	10 46	14 45	17 34
15	18 59	23 52	2 08	10 20	14 27	17 39
Sep 1	29 49	27 35	1 07	9 59	14 09	17 54
15	8♎53	0♍35	0 31	9 51	14 01	18 12
Oct 1	19 25	3 52	0 12	9 54	14 00	18 40
15	28 47	6 33	0 16	10 07	14 05	19 10
Nov 1	10♏22	9 27	0 48	10 36	14 20	19 49
15	20 04	11 28	1 34	11 09	14 39	20 22
Dec 1	1♐21	13 14	2 46	11 55	15 07	21 01
15	11♐24	14♍14	4♒03	12♑41	15♑35	21♏32

1992	♂	♃	♄	♅	♆	♇
Jan 1	23♐47	14♍38	5♒51	13♑41	16♑13	22♏06
15	4♑09	14 16	7 28	14 31	16 45	22 28
Feb 1	16 55	13 01	9 29	15 29	17 22	22 47
15	27 34	11 29	11 09	16 14	17 50	22 56
Mar 1	9♒04	9 33	12 52	16 54	18 16	22 57
15	19 52	7 46	14 21	17 25	18 36	22 51
Apr 1	3♓02	5 58	15 55	17 50	18 51	22 35
15	13 53	5 01	16 59	18 00	18 57	22 17
May 1	26 14	4 38	17 52	17 59	18 56	21 52
15	6♈58	4 56	18 20	17 48	18 48	21 29
Jun 1	19 50	6 04	18 29	17 23	18 31	21 01
15	0♉15	7 32	18 15	16 55	18 13	20 41
Jul 1	11 55	9 44	17 37	16 19	17 48	20 23
15	21 51	12 01	16 48	15 45	17 26	20 13
Aug 1	3♊32	15 08	15 37	15 06	16 59	20 09
15	12 45	17 56	14 34	14 39	16 40	20 13
Sep 1	23 23	21 30	13 23	14 15	16 22	20 26
15	1♋33	24 30	12 36	14 04	16 14	20 45
Oct 1	10 05	27 58	12 01	14 04	16 11	21 12
15	16 36	0♎56	11 49	14 15	16 16	21 40
Nov 1	22 56	4 23	12 02	14 41	16 30	22 19
15	26 22	7 01	12 34	15 12	16 49	22 52
Dec 1	27 36	9 43	13 33	15 56	17 16	23 31
15	25♋50	11♎41	14♒41	16♑41	17♑44	24♏02

1993	♂	♃	♄	♅	♆	♇
Jan 1	20♋25	13♎29	16♒21	17♑40	18♑21	24♏37
15	14 56	14 23	17 53	18 30	18 53	25 00
Feb 1	10 00	14 41	19 53	19 29	19 31	25 20
15	8 41	14 14	21 34	20 14	19 59	25 29
Mar 1	9 46	13 13	23 14	20 54	20 24	25 31
15	12 49	11 44	24 50	21 27	20 44	25 27
Apr 1	18 23	9 36	26 36	21 55	21 01	25 13
15	24 05	7 51	27 52	22 08	21 08	24 55
May 1	1♌27	6 11	29 02	22 11	21 08	24 31
15	8 27	5 12	29 46	22 03	21 01	24 08
Jun 1	17 28	4 45	0♓15	21 41	20 46	23 40
15	25 15	5 03	0 19	21 16	20 28	23 19
Jul 1	4♍28	6 03	29♒59	20 40	20 04	23 00
15	12 45	7 28	29 23	20 07	19 41	22 49
Aug 1	23 07	9 45	28 21	19 27	19 14	22 43
15	1♎52	12 01	27 20	18 58	18 55	22 46
Sep 1	12 45	15 08	26 03	18 31	18 36	22 58
15	21 55	17 56	25 06	18 18	18 26	23 15
Oct 1	2♏38	21 17	24 15	18 14	18 23	23 41
15	12 14	24 19	23 47	18 21	18 26	24 08
Nov 1	24 08	28 00	23 39	18 44	18 39	24 46
15	4♐09	0♏59	23 54	19 12	18 57	25 19
Dec 1	15 50	4 15	24 36	19 54	19 23	25 58
15	26♐14	6♏54	25♒32	20♑37	19♑51	26♏30

1994	♂	♃	♄	♅	♆	♇
Jan 1	9♑04	9♏46	27♒00	21♑35	20♑28	27♏05
15	19 48	11 43	28 26	22 24	20 59	27 29
Feb 1	2♒59	13 30	0♓21	23 24	21 37	27 50
15	13 56	14 22	2 02	24 10	22 06	28 01
Mar 1	24 55	14 39	3 44	24 52	22 32	28 04
15	5♓56	14 20	5 24	25 27	22 53	28 01
Apr 1	19 16	13 10	7 20	25 58	23 11	27 49
15	0♈12	11 42	8 46	26 14	23 19	27 32
May 1	12 34	9 42	10 11	26 21	23 21	27 09
15	23 15	7 58	11 10	26 16	23 15	26 46
Jun 1	6♉01	6 11	12 00	25 58	23 00	26 18
15	16 21	5 12	12 21	25 34	22 43	25 57
Jul 1	27 54	4 46	12 21	25 00	22 20	25 37
15	7♊47	5 01	12 01	24 27	21 57	25 24
Aug 1	19 28	6 04	11 13	23 47	21 30	25 17
15	28 49	7 30	10 19	23 16	21 10	25 18
Sep 1	9♋47	9 48	9 04	22 47	20 50	25 28
15	18 27	12 06	8 01	22 31	20 40	25 44
Oct 1	27 55	15 04	6 56	22 23	20 34	26 09
15	5♌43	17 54	6 13	22 28	20 37	26 35
Nov 1	14 25	21 32	5 44	22 46	20 49	27 12
15	20 45	24 37	5 42	23 12	21 05	27 45
Dec 1	26 46	28 09	6 05	23 51	21 31	28 24
15	0♍34	1♐12	6♓46	24♑32	21♑58	28♏56

1995	♂	♃	♄	♅	♆	♇
Jan 1	2♍39	4♐44	7♓59	25♑28	22♑34	29♏32
15	1 42	7 26	9 16	26 17	23 06	29 56
Feb 1	27♌11	10 20	11 04	27 17	23 44	0♐19
15	21 45	12 19	12 42	28 04	24 13	0 31
Mar 1	16 45	13 52	14 23	28 47	24 40	0 36
15	13 46	14 54	16 06	29 24	25 02	0 34
Apr 1	13 29	15 23	18 09	29 59	25 21	0 23
15	15 40	15 06	19 43	0♒18	25 30	0 08
May 1	20 11	14 04	21 21	0 28	25 33	29♏45
15	25 25	12 40	22 34	0 26	25 28	29 23
Jun 1	2♍55	10 35	23 44	0 11	25 15	28 55
15	9 51	8 50	24 22	29♑50	24 59	28 33
Jul 1	18 22	7 07	24 44	29 18	24 36	28 12
15	26 16	6 04	24 41	28 46	24 13	27 59
Aug 1	6♎21	5 32	24 13	28 05	23 46	27 50
15	14 59	5 46	23 31	27 34	23 25	27 50
Sep 1	25 52	6 49	22 22	27 02	23 05	27 58
15	5♏08	8 15	21 19	26 43	22 53	28 12
Oct 1	16 01	10 27	20 06	26 32	22 47	28 36
15	25 49	12 47	19 11	26 33	22 48	29 02
Nov 1	8♐01	16 01	18 22	26 48	22 58	29 38
15	18 19	18 55	18 02	27 11	23 14	0♐10
Dec 1	0♑19	22 26	18 04	27 47	23 38	0 48
15	11♑00	25♐36	18♓28	28♑26	24♑05	1♐21

1996	♂	♃	♄	♅	♆	♇
Jan 1	24♑10	29♐29	19♓24	29♑21	24♑41	1♐57
15	5♒08	2♑37	20 28	0♒09	25 12	2 23
Feb 1	18 32	6 16	22 06	1 09	25 51	2 47
15	29 37	9 03	23 38	1 57	26 21	3 00
Mar 1	11♓28	11 44	25 24	2 44	26 49	3 06
15	22 28	13 54	27 08	3 23	27 12	3 05
Apr 1	5♈44	15 56	29 14	4 00	27 32	2 55
15	16 31	17 03	0♈54	4 21	27 42	2 41
May 1	28 40	17 38	2 42	4 34	27 45	2 19
15	9♉09	17 29	4 06	4 34	27 41	1 57
Jun 1	21 38	16 31	5 32	4 22	27 29	1 29
15	1♊42	15 09	6 27	4 03	27 13	1 07
Jul 1	13 00	13 13	7 08	3 32	26 50	0 45
15	22 41	11 26	7 23	3 01	26 28	0 31
Aug 1	4♋11	9 32	7 15	2 20	26 01	0 21
15	13 26	8 25	6 48	1 48	25 40	0 20
Sep 1	24 25	7 50	5 52	1 14	25 18	0 28
15	3♌13	8 02	4 53	0 54	25 06	0 41
Oct 1	13 01	8 59	3 38	0 41	24 59	1 04
15	21 18	10 25	2 35	0 39	25 00	1 29
Nov 1	0♍56	12 48	1 31	0 51	25 09	2 04
15	8 28	15 12	0 55	1 11	25 24	2 36
Dec 1	16 28	18 20	0 37	1 45	25 48	3 14
15	22♍46	21♑19	0♈44	2♒23	26♑14	3♐47

EPHEMERIS

The abbreviated Ephemeris below lists the positions for Mars, Jupiter, Saturn, Uranus, Neptune and Pluto. These positions are listed for the 1st and the 15th of each month. For dates between those listed, simply estimate the Planets position according to the distance traveled during the dates shown.

1997	♂	♃	♄	♅	♆	♇
Jan 1	29♍14	25♑10	1♈20	3♒16	26♑50	4♐23
15	3♎13	28 26	2 11	4 04	27 21	4 50
Feb 1	5 46	2♒26	3 36	5 04	28 00	5 14
15	6 26	5 41	5 00	5 52	28 30	5 28
Mar 1	2 33	8 48	6 35	6 37	28 57	5 35
15	27♍41	11 45	8 16	7 17	29 20	5 35
Apr 1	21 19	15 01	10 23	7 57	29 42	5 27
15	17 47	17 20	12 08	8 21	29 53	5 13
May 1	16 48	19 30	14 03	8 37	29 57	4 52
15	18 27	20 53	15 38	8 40	29 55	4 31
Jun 1	22 56	21 49	17 20	8 32	29 43	4 03
15	28 09	21 54	18 30	8 15	29 28	3 41
Jul 1	5♎22	21 15	19 31	7 47	29 06	3 18
15	12 30	20 05	20 06	7 17	28 44	3 03
Aug 1	22 00	18 06	20 22	6 37	28 17	2 52
15	0♏24	16 18	20 13	6 04	27 55	2 50
Sep 1	11 09	14 15	19 36	5 28	27 33	2 56
15	20 26	12 58	18 47	5 05	27 20	3 07
Oct 1	1♐27	12 11	17 38	4 49	27 12	3 29
15	11 24	12 10	16 32	4 44	27 11	3 53
Nov 1	23 51	13 01	15 15	4 52	27 20	4 27
15	4♑21	14 22	14 24	5 09	27 33	4 59
Dec 1	16 35	16 33	13 45	5 40	27 56	5 36
15	27♑27	18♒55	13♈32	6♒16	28♑21	6♐09

1998	♂	♃	♄	♅	♆	♇
Jan 1	10♒46	22♒15	13♈45	7♒07	28♑57	6♐46
15	21 48	25 16	14 19	7 54	29 28	7 13
Feb 1	5♓13	29 11	15 26	8 53	0♒07	7 39
15	16 12	2♓21	16 40	9 42	0 37	7 51
Mar 1	27 09	5 53	18 06	10 28	1 05	8 02
15	7♈58	9 14	19 41	11 10	1 29	8 03
Apr 1	20 57	13 11	21 46	11 52	1 51	7 56
15	1♉28	16 16	23 32	12 19	2 04	7 44
May 1	13 17	19 32	25 33	12 38	2 10	7 24
15	23 27	22 05	27 15	12 44	2 08	7 03
Jun 1	5♊34	24 41	29 09	12 40	1 58	6 35
15	15 21	26 21	0♉33	12 25	1 44	6 13
Jul 1	26 21	27 35	1 53	12 00	1 22	5 50
15	5♋48	28 03	2 46	11 31	1 01	5 34
Aug 1	17 06	27 45	3 26	10 51	0 33	5 21
15	26 15	26 49	3 38	10 18	0 11	5 18
Sep 1	7♌11	25 01	3 24	9 41	29♑49	5 22
15	16 02	23 12	2 51	9 16	29 34	5 33
Oct 1	26 00	21 08	1 54	8 56	29 25	5 52
15	4♍33	19 36	0 51	8 49	29 23	6 15
Nov 1	14 45	18 26	29♈30	8 53	29 30	6 49
15	22 56	18 10	28 28	9 07	29 43	7 20
Dec 1	2♎00	18 41	27 30	9 35	0♒05	7 57
15	9♎38	19♓49	26♈58	10♒08	0♒29	8♐30

1999	♂	♃	♄	♅	♆	♇
Jan 1	18♎23	21♓56	26♈46	10♒57	1♒04	9♐07
15	25 02	24 12	27 01	11 43	1 35	9 35
Feb 1	2♏10	27 27	27 47	12 42	2 13	10 02
15	6 59	0♈26	28 45	13 31	2 44	10 17
Mar 1	10 27	3 36	0♉00	14 18	3 13	10 27
15	12 08	6 55	1 27	15 01	3 37	10 30
Apr 1	11 04	11 01	3 26	15 45	4 01	10 24
15	7 33	14 23	5 10	16 14	4 14	10 13
May 1	1 46	18 11	7 12	16 37	4 22	9 54
15	27♎11	21 22	8 59	16 46	4 21	9 33
Jun 1	24 31	24 59	11 03	16 45	4 12	9 06
15	25 11	27 42	12 37	16 34	3 59	8 43
Jul 1	28 42	0♉24	14 13	16 11	3 38	8 20
15	3♏37	2 21	15 23	15 44	3 17	8 03
Aug 1	11 21	4 03	16 27	15 05	2 49	7 49
15	18 49	4 49	16 59	14 32	2 27	7 44
Sep 1	28 52	4 54	17 11	13 53	2 04	7 47
15	7♐49	4 16	16 57	13 26	1 49	7 56
Oct 1	18 38	2 49	16 18	13 04	1 38	8 15
15	28 31	1 06	15 26	12 53	1 35	8 36
Nov 1	10♑55	28♈49	14 09	12 54	1 41	9 09
15	21 26	27 06	13 01	13 05	1 52	9 39
Dec 1	3♒36	25 41	11 50	13 30	2 13	10 16
15	14♒24	25♈04	11♉01	14♒00	2♒37	10♐49

2000	♂	♃	♄	♅	♆	♇
Jan 1	27♒35	25♈14	10♉24	14♒47	3♒11	11♐27
15	8♓26	26 06	10 18	15 31	3 41	11 54
Feb 1	21 33	27 57	10 39	16 29	4 20	12 22
15	2♈15	0♉01	11 20	17 18	4 51	12 39
Mar 1	13 36	2 40	12 24	18 09	5 22	12 51
15	24 03	5 28	13 41	18 53	5 47	12 54
Apr 1	6♉32	9 11	15 30	19 40	6 12	12 49
15	16 40	12 24	17 10	20 10	6 25	12 39
May 1	28 02	16 10	19 11	20 35	6 33	12 20
15	7♊49	19 30	20 59	20 47	6 34	12 00
Jun 1	19 30	23 30	23 08	20 48	6 26	11 33
15	28 59	26 41	24 51	20 39	6 13	11 11
Jul 1	9♋40	0♊09	26 39	20 18	5 53	10 47
15	18 53	2 56	28 02	19 53	5 32	10 30
Aug 1	29 58	5 57	29 25	19 15	5 04	10 15
15	8♌59	8 01	0♊16	18 42	4 42	10 10
Sep 1	19 51	9 55	0 52	18 02	4 18	10 11
15	28 44	10 53	0 58	17 34	4 02	10 20
Oct 1	8♍48	11 14	0 40	17 10	3 51	10 37
15	17 33	10 50	0 03	16 57	3 47	10 58
Nov 1	28 06	9 31	28♉57	16 54	3 52	11 30
15	6♎43	7 54	27 52	17 03	4 03	12 00
Dec 1	16 27	5 45	26 34	17 25	4 23	12 36
15	24♎53	3♊56	25♉32	17♒54	4♒46	13♐09

Readings by the Author

The Author welcomes you to call for a *private consultations* (via phone or in person). For further information, please call (916) 326-0402. Leave your name and both a day and evening telephone number.

"THE WORKS"

A Special Package
Designed Specifically for This Book.

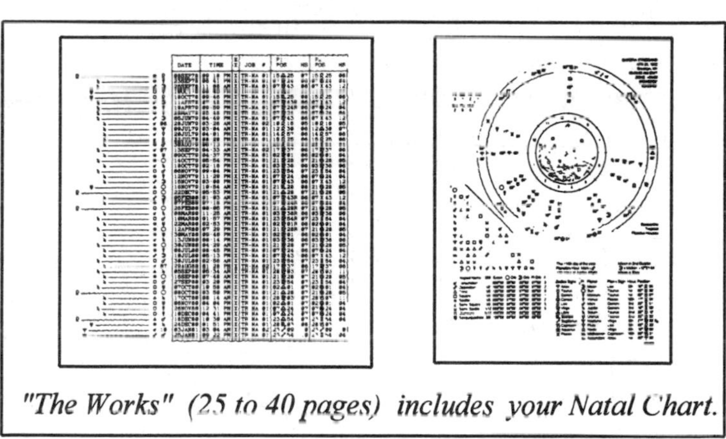

"The Works" (25 to 40 pages) includes your Natal Chart.

*Save hours of time looking up your Transits and turn your study into a real joy. Order **"The Works"**!*

"The Works" is a 25 to 40 page personalized Ephemeris customized to your Birth Chart. It gives the exact date and time of all major events in your Natal Chart starting from when you were ten years old to ten years from the date of your order. As a personalized reference tool, this customized document can be used throughout your Astrological studies and predictions for the next ten years.

COST ONLY - $27.00

(To order "The Works", see next page.)

NATAL CHARTS

"THE WORKS"

"The Works" is a special package designed specifically for this book. Each order includes a 25 to 40 page custom Ephemeris beginning at age ten and ending ten years from the date of order. It includes the date & time for all Major Aspects made to your Chart by Transiting Jupiter, Saturn, Uranus, Neptune & Pluto as well as Conjunctions made to your Houses. In addition, your Birth Chart is included free.

"THE WORKS"

Name: ____________________

____

Mo/Da/Yr: ____________________

Time: ______________ am/pm

City: ____________________

State: ____________________

NATAL CHARTS

All Natal Charts are calculated according to the Placidus House System, which is recommended by the Author. If you do not have your exact birth time, 12:00 pm will be used.

NATAL CHARTS

Name: ____________________

____

Mo/Da/Yr: ____________________

Time: ______________ am/pm

City: ____________________

State: ____________________

Name: ____________________

____

Mo/Da/Yr: ____________________

Time: ______________ am/pm

City: ____________________

State: ____________________

For additional Charts etc., use a separate sheet of paper.

"The Works" ___ x $27 ea = ________

Charts ___ x $4 ea = ________

Mars Cycle (*see page 84*) ___ x $6 ea = ________

P&H $1.50 per order = $1.50

(*Foreign orders*: Add $3.50 to total.) TOTAL = ________

Mail cash, check or money order to: **TEC Publications, 4511 - Del Rio Road #5, Sacramento, CA 95822.**